Let Me Tell You
What I Mean

Let Me Tell You What I Mean

Joan Didion

Foreword by Hilton Als

Alfred A. Knopf
New York
2021

THIS IS A BORZOI BOOK
PUBLISHED BY ALFRED A. KNOPF

www.aaknopf.com

Knopf, Borzoi Books, and the colophon
are registered trademarks of Penguin Random House LLC.

Grateful acknowledgment is made to the following for permission to
reprint previously published materials:
Little, Brown and Company: "Some Women" originally published as
the introduction to *Some Women* by Robert Mapplethorpe.
Introduction copyright © 1989 by Joan Didion. Reprinted by permission of
Little, Brown and Company, an imprint of Hachette Book Group, Inc.
HarperCollins Publishers: "The Long-Distance Runner" originally published
as the introduction to *The Long-Distance Runner* by Tony Richardson.
Introduction copyright © 1993 by Joan Didion. Reprinted by
permission of HarperCollins Publishers.

A shortened version of "Pretty Nancy" later appeared in *The White Album* (1979).
"Why I Write" later appeared in the anthology *The Writer on Her Work*,
edited by Janet Sternberg and first published in 1980.

The following essays first appeared in the *Saturday Evening Post*:
"Alicia and the Underground Press," "Getting Serenity," "A Trip to Xanadu,"
"On Being Unchosen by the College of One's Choice," "Pretty Nancy," "Fathers,
Sons, Screaming Eagles." "Why I Write" first appeared in *The New York Times
Magazine;* "Telling Stories" first appeared in *New West;* "Last Words" and
"Everywoman.com" first appeared in *The New Yorker.*

Library of Congress Cataloging-in-Publication Data
Names: Didion, Joan, author.
Title: Let me tell you what I mean / Joan Didion; foreword by Hilton Als.
Description: First edition. | New York : Alfred A. Knopf, [2021] | "This is
a Borzoi Book published by Alfred A. Knopf"—Title page verso. |
Identifiers: LCCN 2020016867 (print) | LCCN 2020016868 (ebook) |
ISBN 9780593318485 (hardcover) | ISBN 9780593318492 (ebook)
Classification: LCC PS3554.I33 A6 2021 (print) | LCC PS3554.I33 (ebook) |
DDC 814/.54—dc23
LC record available at https://lccn.loc.gov/2020016867
LC ebook record available at https://lccn.loc.gov/20200168

Jacket design by Carol Devine Carson

Manufactured in the United States of America
Published January 26, 2021
Reprinted One Time
Third Printing, February 2021

Contents

A peculiar aspect of Joan Didion's nonfiction is that a significant portion of it reads like fiction. Or, more specifically, has the metaphorical power of great fiction. While younger generations may read the master as a kind of window into the mythical 1960s, or 9/11, say, it's impossible not to see, too, how Didion's examination of racial bias and the Central Park Five, Reagan-era El Salvador, or the smug, violent, white male carelessness that characterized the infamous Spur Posse in Lakewood, California, in the early 1990s, anticipated the deeply troubling politics of today. And while the farsighted Didion is certainly in evidence in a few of her early essays collected in this book of twelve previously uncollected pieces—essays ranging from a 1968 report on Gamblers Anony-

mous to an appreciation of Martha Stewart, published thirty-two years later—what makes the
early work particularly interesting is how Didion's
now famous cool and shifting perspective takes a
backseat to Didion the Opiner. From 1968's "Alicia
and the Underground Press":

> The only American newspapers that do not
> leave me in the grip of a profound physical
> conviction that the oxygen has been cut off
> from my brain tissue, very probably by an
> Associated Press wire, are *The Wall Street
> Journal,* the Los Angeles *Free Press,* the
> Los Angeles *Open City,* and the *East Village
> Other.* I tell you that not to make myself out
> an amusing eccentric, perverse and eclectic
> and, well, groovy in all her tastes; I am talk-
> ing here about something deadening and
> peculiar, the inability of all of us to speak to
> one another in any direct way, the failure of
> American newspapers to "get through."

This piece is exceptional for a number of reasons, the primary one being, aside from its decid-

edly emphatic, cranky tone and the long-ago days
that titles like the *East Village Other* evoke, is
Didion laying out a kind of writerly ethos a little
further along in the piece.

She says:

> The *Free Press,* the *EVO,* the *Berkeley Barb,*
> all the other tabloid-sized papers that reflect
> the special interests of the young and the
> disaffiliated: their particular virtue is to
> be devoid of conventional press postures,
> so many of which rest on a quite factitious
> "objectivity." Do not misread me: I admire
> objectivity very much indeed, but I fail to
> see how it can be achieved if the reader does
> not understand the writer's particular bias.
> For the writer to pretend that he has none
> lends the entire venture a mendacity that
> has never infected *The Wall Street Journal*
> and does not infect yet the underground
> press. When a writer for an underground
> paper approves or disapproves of some-
> thing, he says so, quite often in lieu of who,
> what, where, when, how.

Of course, part of the remarkable character of Didion's work has to do with her refusal to pretend that she doesn't exist. From the time she began writing for *The Saturday Evening Post* specifically—she and her husband, John Gregory Dunne, shared a column called "Points West" for the magazine from 1964 to 1969—through masterly late novels such as 1984's *Democracy,* Didion has wrestled with the "I" character, which is to say with truth and perspective as it applied to, or appealed to, herself. That she rejected the notion that the world can be filtered through the precepts of journalism and come out on the other side as "true" radicalized Joan Didion's nonfiction from the first. Her narrative nonfiction is a question about the truth. And if her nonfiction is synonymous with anything, says Didion in work after work, it is with the idea that the truth is provisional, and the only thing backing it up is who you are at the time you wrote this or that, and that your joys and biases and prejudices are part of writing, too. And while a few of these pieces were written around the time Didion published some of her justly famous reporting as well—her landmark collection, *Slouching Towards Bethlehem,* came out in 1968—it was Didion's fiction that taught her, I think, how to articulate what bugged her by tempering it with humor and a dry little sigh of exasperation. In novels like 1970's *Play It as It Lays,* and her early masterpiece, 1977's *A Book of Common Prayer,* the intensities of youth were replaced with the rueful forbearance of the experienced woman who could create protagonists and narrators who had seen their share of stuff go down, or not happen, or whatever. Didion the novelist taught Didion the nonfiction writer.

When you read a writer in a popular magazine or newspaper, you are getting two writers, really. There's the person who has something to say, and the person who has to make that something fit. The "Points West" columns were, for the most part, limited by space. Didion had roughly two thousand words for the column, and she had to use them to tell the story of what she saw, felt, thought, which means that sometimes she used didacticism as a tool. And yet even then Didion could right an ideological wrong in her own thinking by not turning away from mystery.

While "Getting Serenity" is ostensibly about some
folks who are wrestling with gambling addic-
tions, the piece is filled with Didion's implicit
disdain for anything that smacks of "self-help,"
combined with her (again implicit) up-by-your-
bootstraps-don't-complain-and-don't-look-back
California ethos. "There was nothing particularly
wrong" about the meetings, she writes, "and yet
there was something not quite right, something
troubling. At first I thought that it was simply the
predilection of many of the members to dwell on
how 'powerless' they were." In the end, though,
Didion finally recognizes what she finds troubling. Frank L., one of the gamblers Didion writes
about, is celebrating a year of sobriety with his
family and friends. There's a cake. "It hasn't been
easy," he says to the assembled. "But in the last
three, four weeks we've gotten a . . . a *serenity* at
home." Then:

> Well, there it was. I got out fast then, before
> anyone could say "serenity" again, for it is a
> word I associate with death, and for several
> days after that meeting I wanted only to be

in places where the lights were bright and
no one counted days.

That an author could be undone by the story
she was telling wasn't especially new in 1968;
Norman Mailer, a Didion favorite, had, that very
year, published *The Armies of the Night,* his report
on antiwar activism in and around Washington.
But Mailer had narrated his book as "Mailer," a
third-person character who, despite his extrava-
gant personality, was a few steps removed from
his material. In the early essays collected here,
Didion is saying that a woman's "I"—her eye
and I—didn't need any such devices to tell the
story; what Didion needed was a situation that
provoked a reaction and gave her her story, in
all senses of the word. The existential crisis she
experiences at the end of "Getting Serenity" is a
great example of that, and a great example of how
language affects the writer who loves words but
knows how they can undo us, too. When I first
started reading Didion in the late 1970s, it became
clear to me after a while that one of her big subjects was the craft of writing itself. Why it mat-

tered to her, mattered to anyone, and it's writing as
subject, writing as a way of life, that is part of this
book. She has a great deal to say about the craft
in her 1998 essay about Ernest Hemingway, parts
of which feel like a self-portrait of Joan Didion
herself.

> The very grammar of a Hemingway sen-
> tence dictated, or was dictated by, a certain
> way of looking at the world, a way of look-
> ing but not joining, a way of moving through
> but not attaching, a kind of romantic indi-
> vidualism distinctly adapted to its time and
> source.

*A way of looking but not joining, a way of mov-
ing through but not attaching*—certainly these are
the qualities I found so striking in Didion's nonfiction, but what further set her writing apart from
Hemingway's now very dated "romantic individu-
alism" was the physics or energy in Didion's writing, what she might call its "shimmer." And it's that
energy or shimmer that sheds a sort of awful and
beautiful light on a world we half see but don't
want to see, one where potential harm is a given,

the bogeyman may be your father, and hope is a flimsy defense against dread. Indeed, what Didion alone brings to contemporary nonfiction is a feeling for the uncanny. In his 1919 essay about the phenomenon, Freud writes that the uncanny is synonymous with and expressive of "all that arouses dread and creeping horror." But the good doctor observes in the same paper that "the word itself is not always used in a clearly definable sense, so that it tends to coincide with whatever excites dread." Part of Didion's brilliance is not so much to define menace or the uncanny as to show it. Take, for instance, a scene that has stayed with me since I first read *Slouching Towards Bethlehem,* Didion's 1967 report on San Francisco's Haight-Ashbury youth culture and drug scene. One afternoon the author finds herself sitting with some of her subjects in the city's Panhandle.

Janis Joplin is singing with Big Brother . . . and almost everybody is high and it is a pretty nice Sunday afternoon . . . and who turns up but Peter Berg. He is with his wife and six or seven other people . . . and the first peculiar thing is, they're in blackface.

I mention to Max and Sharon that some members of the Mime Troupe seem to be in blackface.

"It's street theater," Sharon assures me. "It's supposed to be really groovy."

The Mime Troupers get a little closer, and there are some other peculiar things about them. For one thing they are tapping people on the head with dime-store plastic nightsticks, and for another they are wearing signs on their backs. "HOW MANY TIMES HAVE YOU BEEN RAPED, YOU LOVE FREAKS?" and "WHO STOLE CHUCK BERRY'S MUSIC?," things like that. Then they are distributing communication company fliers which say:

> & this summer thousands of un-white un-suburban boppers are going to want to know why you've given up what they can't get & how you get away with it . . .

Max reads the flier and stands up. "I'm getting bad vibes," he says, and he and Sharon leave.

I have to stay around because I'm looking

for Otto so I walk over to where the Mime Troupers have formed a circle around a Negro. Peter Berg is saying if anybody asks that this is street theater, and I figure the curtain is up because what they are doing right now is jabbing the Negro with the nightsticks. They jab, and they bare their teeth, and they rock on the balls of their feet and they wait.

"I'm beginning to get annoyed here," the Negro says. "I'm gonna get mad."

By now there are several Negroes around, reading the signs and watching.

"Just beginning to get annoyed, are you?" one of the Mime Troupers says. "Don't you think it's about time?" . . .

"Listen," the Negro says, his voice rising. "You're gonna start something here, this isn't right—"

"You tell us what's right, black boy," the girl says.

For the black man at the center of this particular drama, the horror that is visited upon him and his good time in the park is further proof of the

"dread and creeping horror" that his skin color
generates in the white world. For her part, Didion
is not herself during this exchange—a dominant
"I." Unlike other nonfiction writers she admires,
Graham Greene among them, Didion doesn't
insert her personality in the scene; she can't edi-
torialize, or won't, because, to her, nightmares
carry their own weight, and it's the writer's job to
be awake when the nightmare or uncanny happens. Because it will. Didion's ethos is not much
related to a school but a way of seeing that's particular to who she is, to the world that made her,
a way of seeing that, ultimately, reveals the writer
to herself.

We are all from somewhere. And it's the artist's job to question the values that went into the
making of that somewhere. What you'll notice
in Didion's nonfiction as well is how her famous
clarity becomes even sharper when disquiet rat-
tles the cage of the quotidian, or she's in the presence of indefensible bodies, which is to say that
man in the Panhandle. Who will protect him?
"Society"? Didion shows us how much society
cares by recording the self-protective, which is

to say the ultimately self-interested language of the Haight—"I'm getting bad vibes"—as a way of showing how little responsibility the children are willing to take on. (It was only a year after the book's publication that Meredith Hunter, another black man, was killed by Hells Angel Alan Passaro during the Rolling Stones' free concert at Altamont.) Why was Joan Didion there in the first place? "I'm not interested in the middle road—maybe because everyone's on it," Didion said in a 1979 interview with the critic Michiko Kakutani. "Rationality, reasonableness bewilder me.... A lot of the stories I was brought up on had to do with extreme actions—leaving everything behind, crossing the trackless wastes ..."

In the America that the now eighty-six-year-old Joan Didion, a fifth-generation Californian, grew up in—middle class, Protestant, Republican Sacramento—the social mores were fixed, intractable. You didn't make a show of yourself, and what you said was probably less complicated than what you thought. Postwar prosperity was a given. But how it was acquired was another story altogether. Sacramento—Spanish for "sacrament"—

was built on a swamp; the valley depended on
federal handouts in order to expand, and some
private citizens and corporations who got in on
those transactions profited. In short, Sacramento
wasn't so much "discovered" as manufactured.

Didion didn't know any of that when she was
a kid growing up in that hot-and-dry-in-the-
summer or rainy-in-the-winter-and-early-spring
Eden, complete with snakes. As a kid she was fed
a steady diet of myths—the rugged individual
myth, the Western arrival myth. Didion's mother,
Eduene Jerrett, had worked as a librarian before
marrying Frank Didion, who supported his family,
variously, as an Army Corps officer, by selling in-
surance, gambling, and as a real estate developer.
Eduene was the more verbal of the two, and it was
she who told Joan stories that fed her daughter's
imagination. One story concerned Nancy Har-
din Cornwall and Josephus Adamson Cornwall,
pioneer ancestors who, along with their progeny,
split off from the Donner-Reed Party at the Hum-
boldt Sink in Nevada to cut north through Oregon,
thus escaping the death and cannibalism the sur-
viving party suffered. And it was Eduene who gave

five-year-old Joan a Big Tablet pad so she'd stop
complaining and write down what was troubling
her. (Didion's younger brother, Jim, was born
in 1939.) As a member of a reasonably successful and connected clan with roots that ran deep
on both sides in clannish Sacramento—Frank's
great-great-grandfather, for instance, had immi-
grated to Sacramento from Ohio in 1855—Didion
learned early on how cut off its valley citizens were
from the larger world. But was it a problem? "My
mother made the trip from Sacramento to Los
Angeles in 1932, to see the Olympics, and did not
find reason to make it again for thirty years," reports Didion in her 2003 book, *Where I Was From.*
And as a young woman, the author recalls visiting
a rancher's widow with her mother. The woman
was, Didion writes in her 1965 essay "Notes from
a Native Daughter"—which appeared in Didion's
first collection, *Slouching Towards Bethlehem*—
"reminiscing (the favored conversational mode
in Sacramento) about the son of some contem-
poraries of hers. 'That Johnson boy never did
amount to much,' she said. Desultorily, my mother
protested: Alva Johnson, she said, had won the

Pulitzer Prize, when he was working for *The New York Times*. Our hostess looked at us impassively. 'He never amounted to anything in Sacramento,' she said." What mattered in Sacramento: history, but only as it pertained to Sacramento or arriving in Sacramento and putting down stakes and staying put. Also from "Notes from a Native Daughter":

> It is characteristic of Californians to speak grandly of the past as if it had simultaneously begun, *tabula rasa,* and reached a happy ending on the day the wagons started west. *Eureka*—"I Have Found It"—as the state motto has it. Such a view of history casts a certain melancholia over those who participate in it; my own childhood was suffused with the conviction that we had long outlived our finest hour.... If I could make you understand that, I could make you understand California and perhaps something else besides, for Sacramento *is* California, and California is a place in which a boom mentality and a sense of Chekhovian

loss meet in uneasy suspension; in which the mind is troubled by some buried but ineradicable suspicion that things had better work here, because here, beneath that immense bleached sky, is where we run out of continent.

One way children hold on to the edge of the world is by believing that they're at the center of it. Could be in California, could be anywhere. Inevitably, as one grows, one begins to see that the distance between where you stand on solid ground and falling off the edge of the world altogether is mighty narrow indeed, and that you and other people, not to mention your parents, are cracked and lonely because we all are. Didion's father had a troubled mind—he suffered from depression. Like any number of the forlorn male characters in Chekhov, not to mention the catch-as-catch-can, often absent husbands and fathers in Didion's last three novels—*A Book of Common Prayer* (1977), *Democracy* (1984), and *The Last Thing He Wanted* (1996)—Frank had no real ability to describe what he felt, let alone to his family.

If Eduene Didion could talk, Frank Didion had silence, which comes with its own kind of power, as Didion notes in *Where I Was From* (2003). Language belonged to his daughter.

> There was about him a sadness so pervasive that it colored even those many moments when he seemed to be having a good time. He had many friends. He played golf, he played tennis, he played poker, he seemed to enjoy parties. Yet he could be in the middle of a party at our own house, sitting at the piano—playing "Darktown Strutter's Ball," say, or "Alexander's Ragtime Band," a bourbon highball always within reach—and the tension he transmitted would seem so great that I would have to leave, run to my room and close the door.

It takes a long time to tell the truth; Didion worked on *Where I Was From* in various forms for many years. It was only after her parents died that she was able to complete it. In *The Uncanny,* Freud points out that

the uncanny of real experience has far simpler determinants, but comprises fewer
instances. I believe that it invariably . . . can
be traced back every time to something that
was once familiar and then repressed. . . .
Where the uncanny stems from childhood
complexes, the question of material reality
does not arise, its place being taken by psychical reality. Here we are dealing with the
actual repression of a particular content and
the return of what has been repressed, not
with the suspension of *belief in its reality.*

The repression of Frank's "content." How did
this affect Didion before she had the language to
describe it? Did it cause the high school student
who loved Hemingway and Joseph Conrad—
writers who delved, again and again, into the
failure of love, and romance as a dream that
curdled the soul, or left one to be just a trace of
one's former self, whoever that was—to long for a
different psychical reality, one that wasn't shored
up by highballs and land values and community
boards, a guy who basically said fuck it to what

Sacramento society deemed correct and followed another path altogether? Guys like that didn't fit in and didn't want to fit in; they were nothing like the men Didion knew at home. Such guys, Didion writes in her 1988 essay "Insider Baseball," didn't go to "Yale or Swarthmore or DePauw, nor had they even applied." Indeed,

> [t]hey had gotten drafted, gone through basic at Fort Ord. They had knocked up girls, and married them, had begun what they called the first night of the rest of their lives with a midnight drive to Carson City and a five-dollar ceremony performed by a justice of the peace still in his pajamas. They got jobs at the places that had laid off their uncles. . . . They were never destined to be, in other words, communicants in what we have come to call, when we want to indicate the traditional ways in which power is exchanged and the status quo maintained in the United States, "the process."

The traditional ways in which power is exchanged and the status quo maintained. Again and again throughout her career, Didion has struggled with the idea, let alone the reality, of what makes the status quo, what constitutes tradition, and how the visiting "bad boy" or unforeseen event disrupts the world as people like the Didions, or the people they associated with in Sacramento, knew it. One way those bad boys made a world different was through sex or, more accurately, the projection of sex. John Wayne, whom Didion first saw in the pictures when she was a kid—"He had a sexual authority so strong that even a child could perceive it"—continued to draw the adult woman writer to him in part because he seemed to come from out of nowhere, and had a history that "was no history at all," meaning no biography could explain him. Jim Morrison of the Doors came out of nowhere, too, and with a definite point of view or aura as well— "The Doors were the Norman Mailers of the Top Forty, missionaries of apocalyptic sex," Didion wrote in 1979's *The White Album*. But what would the words to the song mean without the singer? It was Morrison, Didion insists, who got up there in his "black vinyl pants and no underwear," while tending to "suggest some range of the possible just beyond a suicide pact," and sold the band's ethos—sex as the ultimate high, and transgression. Didion was also drawn to more traditional writers who gave off a similar energy on the page, guys who reported on their extreme states of consciousness in story after story littered with sex and death and what goes wrong when the status quo is undone by forces it can't control. Didion in high school, hanging out with guys who didn't bother with college, Didion observing Frank at the piano, or watching John Wayne onscreen as a kid, selling sexuality—all of this is fascinating in part because it's rare: as a woman looking at men and not looking away, Joan Didion reversed the standard male-female deal, while developing the Didion gaze.

In 1952, the burgeoning writer was admitted to the University of California at Berkeley, where she majored in English. Berkeley was not her first choice. She had applied to Stanford, but had not gotten in, a disappointment she writes about in her 1968 piece "On Being Unchosen by the College of One's Choice." In it, Didion describes the day she received her letter of rejection:

> I remember quite clearly the afternoon I opened that letter. I stood reading and rereading it, my sweater and my books fallen on the hall floor, trying to interpret the words in some less final way, the phrases "unable to take" and "favorable action" fading in and out of focus until the sentence made no sense at all. We lived then in a big dark Victorian house, and I had a sharp and dolorous image of myself growing old in it, never going to school anywhere, the spinster in *Washington Square.*

Throughout her writing life, Joan Didion has held on to that letter, not only to remember who she was, but how things don't work out, and shouldn't work out, not always: it's dashed expectations that dislodge you from being fixed in outlook, fixed in what you feel you "deserve," and how getting into Stanford, or Yale, or Harvard, often has something to do with following someone else's script. The parent script. The family script. It's safe to assume that, by the time Didion got to Berkeley, she wasn't following anyone else's script, but that doesn't mean she didn't want to learn the lines she thought she needed to know in order to get by. The Bay Area that Didion landed in in the early 1950s was, to use the parlance of the time, culturally speaking, mostly "nowhere." Abstract Expressionism, for instance—the combustive, ragged, and elegant art form that caused the art world to turn its attention away from Europe to America—blossomed in New York, not Marin County. At Berkeley, Didion discovered she didn't know how to think, certainly as thinking was defined at the university.

From her 1975 lecture "Why I Write":

> During the years when I was an undergradu-
> ate at Berkeley I tried, with a kind of hope-
> less late-adolescent energy, to buy some
> temporary visa into the world of ideas, to
> forge myself a mind that could deal with the
> abstract.
>
> In short I tried to think. . . . My attention
> veered inexorably back to the specific, to the

tangible, to what was generally considered, by everyone I knew then and for that matter have known since, the peripheral. I would try to contemplate the Hegelian dialectic and would find myself concentrating instead on a flowering pear tree outside my window and the particular way the petals fell on my floor. I would try to read linguistic theory and would find myself wondering instead if the lights were on in the Bevatron up the hill.... [Y]ou might immediately suspect, if you deal in ideas at all, that I was registering the Bevatron as a political symbol ... but you would be wrong. I was only wondering if the lights were on in the Bevatron, and how they looked. A physical fact.

Perhaps Didion couldn't speak Hegelian—or Hegel didn't speak to her—because even then she was already engaged in learning how to speak Californian. Every writer is a regionalist. In a 1979 review of Norman Mailer's *The Executioner's Song,* a book about the Utah native and murderer Gary Gilmore, Didion describes what makes Western speech so difficult to capture. How do you

make a language out of emptiness, "that vast emptiness at the center of the Western experience, a
nihilism not only antithetical to literature but to
most other human forms of endeavor, a dread so
close to zero that human voices fade out, trail off,
like skywriting"? Dread can stymie speech, certainly, but it can also make you wary of the idea of
communicating anything at all. What's the point if
what you feel can't be spoken? Life in Sacramento
taught Didion that.

And yet, how could one's Americanness—itself
an uncanny place: How did we get here? What are
we doing here? Why do we stay?—measure up to
all those linguistic theorists? (We are all linguistic
theorists if we deal with language at all. But try
telling that to a seventeen-year-old overachiever.)
How could California, as subject and reality, measure up to the Europe Hemingway, for instance,
mined in his fiction? Was Europe a "thing" she
had to consider if she was going to write her
world? Did she want to write the entire world? Or
would her Americanness—her Didionness—be
enough? Those are questions that got deeper,
and Didion tried to look at more closely, and, ulti-

mately, to answer for herself after she finished at Berkeley, moved to New York, and began working at *Vogue*. In New York, the girl who had grown up near and in rivers found herself walking to the East River because she missed what she knew, and the only way to capture it was by writing; Didion's first novel, 1963's *Run River*, is as much as anything an act of memory, and memorialization.

But we are getting ahead of her story. I think it's safe to say that Didion, a carver of words in the granite of the specific, might have been less than inspired by the Cold War writing that was popular on both coasts when she was a college student; in any case, it's hard to imagine her as a Dharma bum. Too much posturing there. What Didion sought was naturalness of expression as controlled by a true understanding of one's craft, the better to describe the ineffable, the uncanny in the everyday. But how would she achieve that? By the act of writing, being a writer. In 1954, when she was nineteen, Didion was accepted into the late Mark Schorer's English 106A, an experience Didion describes in her 1978 reminiscence "Telling Stories." The class, she says was "a kind of 'writers'

workshop' which met for discussion three hours
a week and required that each student produce,
over the course of the semester, at least five short
stories. No auditors were allowed.... English
106A was widely regarded in the fall of 1954 as a
kind of sacramental experience, an initiation into
the grave world of real writers, and I remember
each meeting of this class as an occasion of acute
excitement and dread." Didion's dread was based
in part on the feeling that she hadn't experienced
enough to complete five short stories. And it was
dread, too, that made her want to disappear in
class, which, incidentally, she never missed. "I
ransacked my closet for clothes in which I might
appear invisible in class," Didion remembers,
"and came up with only a dirty raincoat. I sat in
this raincoat and I listened to other people's stories read aloud and I despaired of ever knowing
what they knew." As every writer knows, writing
is not inseparable from your body; it's you, you're
the singer and the song. Throughout her career,
Didion has lived or projected an "I" on the page,
while maintaining a certain distance, a desire to
disappear so the pictures and people that make

the story can at least in part tell it. But when Didion was in Mark Schorer's class, she wasn't certain
that the stories she told, wanted to tell, were the
stories people would want to hear. How to disappear in life, and say "I" on the page, all at once. Taking Schorer's class was not greater than her fear
and dread; it was equal to both. That each lives
with the other, seemingly forever—"The peculiarity of being a writer is that the entire enterprise
involves the mortal humiliation of seeing one's
own words in print," says Didion in "Last Words,"
her 1998 essay about Hemingway—is part of the
writing life, which writers somehow manage to
survive, over and over again, in order to write,
which is in itself an exercise in the uncanny.

—Hilton Als
July 2020

Let Me Tell You
What I Mean

Alicia and the Underground Press

The only American newspapers that do not leave me in the grip of a profound physical conviction that the oxygen has been cut off from my brain tissue, very probably by an Associated Press wire, are *The Wall Street Journal,* the Los Angeles *Free Press,* the Los Angeles *Open City,* and the *East Village Other.* I tell you that not to make myself out an amusing eccentric, perverse and eclectic and, well, groovy in all her tastes; I am talking here about something deadening and peculiar, the inability of all of us to speak to one another in any direct way, the failure of American newspapers to "get through." *The Wall Street Journal* talks to me directly (that I have only a minimal interest in much of what it tells me is beside the point), and so does the "underground" press.

The *Free Press,* the *EVO,* the *Berkeley Barb,*
all the other tabloid-sized papers that reflect the
special interests of the young and the disaffiliated:
their particular virtue is to be devoid of conventional press postures, so many of which rest on a
quite factitious "objectivity." Do not misread me:
I admire objectivity very much indeed, but I fail
to see how it can be achieved if the reader does
not understand the writer's particular bias. For the
writer to pretend that he has none lends the entire
venture a mendacity that has never infected *The
Wall Street Journal* and does not yet infect the
underground press. When a writer for an underground paper approves or disapproves of something, he says so, quite often in lieu of who, what,
where, when, how.

Of course there is nothing particularly underground about the underground papers. New York
south of Thirty-fourth Street is papered with the
EVO; Los Angeles accountants pick up the *Free
Press* at lunch on the Strip. It is a commonplace
to complain that the papers are amateurish and
badly written (they are), that they are silly (they
are), that they are boring (they are not), that they

are not sufficiently inhibited by information. In fact, the information content of an underground paper is low in the extreme. News of a peace march or of the defection of a rock group to the forces of exploitation (the group released a record, say, or accepted an engagement to play at Cheetah), advice from Patricia Maginnis on what to tell the admitting intern if you start hemorrhaging after a Mexican abortion ("Feel perfectly free to tell them that Patricia Maginnis and/or Rowena Gurner assisted you to get your abortion. Please don't incriminate anyone else. We are trying to get arrested. Other people aren't"), second thoughts from a fifteen-year-old narcotics dealer ("You have to have a commitment to dealing as a lifestyle, or you can't do it well"), admonitions that Speed Kills: one issue of, say, the *Free Press* is very like the next five issues of the *Free Press,* and, to anyone who follows only casually the various schisms among drug users and guerrilla revolutionaries, indistinguishable from the *EVO,* the *Barb,* the *Fifth Estate,* the Washington *Free Press.* I have never read anything I needed to know in an underground paper.

But to think that these papers are read for "facts" is to misapprehend their appeal. It is the genius of these papers that they talk directly to their readers. They assume that the reader is a friend, that he is disturbed about something, and that he will understand if they talk to him straight; this assumption of a shared language and a common ethic lends their reports a considerable cogency of style. A recent *Free Press* carried an analysis of Ann Arbor by a reader named "Alicia," who said all there was to say about a university community in three lines of haiku-like perfection: "The professors and their wives are ex-Beatniks (Berkeley, Class of '57), and they go on peace marches and bring daffodils to U Thant. Some of the kids still believe in Timothy Leary and Kahlil Gibran. Some of their parents still believe in the Kinsey Report."

These papers ignore the conventional newspaper code, say what they mean. They are strident and brash, but they do not irritate; they have the faults of a friend, not of a monolith. ("Monolith," of course, is a favorite underground-press word, one of the few with three syllables.) Their point of view is clear to the densest reader. In the best of the traditional press there exist very strong unspoken attitudes indeed, and the fact that those attitudes remain unspoken, unadmitted, comes between the page and the reader like so much marsh gas. *The New York Times* brings out in me only unpleasant agrarian aggressions, makes me feel like the barker's barefoot daughter in *Carousel,* watching the Snow children prance off to Sunday dinner with McGeorge Bundy, Reinhold Niebuhr, Dr. Howard Rusk. The cornucopia overflows. The Cross of Gold gleams. The barker's daughter dreams of anarchy and would not trust the Snow children to tell her that last night it was dark. Below the level of the New York or the Los Angeles *Times,* the problem is not so much whether one trusts the news as whether one finds it; quite often a monkey seems to have taken the entire bewildering affair from the teletype, throwing in a totem report here, a press release there. The summer I was seventeen I worked on a paper where the major thrust of each day's effort was to clip and rewrite the opposition paper ("Check it out if it looks like a plant," I was advised my first day); I have the impression that this kind of thing remains a lively local industry: County Board of Supervisors Lauds North Area Realtors for Plan to Raze Slum, Construct Howard Johnson's. Charity-minded Debutantes Inspect Recently Purchased Machine for Treatment of Terminal Cancer. Dear Abby. Mirror of Your Mind. The tongue lolls, reality recedes. "Seminary Sounds Like Boy Needs Dictionary," one reads on page 35. "PADUCAH, KY. (AP)—"When Kay Fowler asked her Sunday-school class to describe a seminary, one little fellow piped up: 'That's where they bury people.'" Tell me that on page 35, and I am not likely to believe you on page one.

Monkeys on the lower levels, code on the higher. It is a comment on our press conventions that we are considered "well-informed" to precisely the extent that we know "the real story," the story not in the newspaper. We have come to expect newspapers to reflect the official ethic, to do the "responsible" thing. The most admired newspapermen are no longer adversaries but confidants, participants; the ideal is to advise Presidents, dine with Walter Reuther and Henry

Ford, and dance with the latter's daughters at Le
Club. And then, heavy with responsibility, to file
their coded reports. Alicia is not long on responsibility. Alicia never goes to Le Club. Alicia probably
doesn't know anything about anything outside of
Ann Arbor. But she tells me all she knows about
that.

1968

Getting Serenity

Speaking for myself," the young woman said, "in the seven months since I been on the program it's been real good. I was strictly a Gardena player, lowball. I'd play in the nighttime after I got my children to bed, and of course I never got home before five a.m., and my *problem* was, I couldn't sleep then. I'd replay every single hand, so the next day I'd be, you know, tired. Irritable. With the children."

Her tone was that of someone who had adapted her mode of public address from analgesic commercials, but she was not exactly selling a product. She was making a "confession" at a meeting of Gamblers Anonymous I attended not long ago: nine o'clock on a winter evening in a bungalow neighborhood clubhouse in Gardena, California.

Gardena is the draw-poker capital of Los Angeles
County (no stud, no alcoholic beverages, clubs
closed between 5:00 a.m. and 9:00 a.m. and all day
on Christmas Day; this is not Nevada but California, where there is only draw poker and that only
on local option), and the seductive proximity of
the poker clubs hung over this particular meeting
like a paraphysical substance, almost as palpable
as the portraits of Washington and Lincoln, the
American flag, the plastic hydrangeas, and the
table laid by the Refreshments Committee. Just
around the corner waiting for someone, there
it was, the action, and there in that overheated
room, shifting uneasily on folding chairs and
blinking against the cigarette smoke, were forty
people who craved it. "This Gardena," a young
man breathed softly. "She destroyed me." The
young man, who said he had done OK in mechanical drawing at Van Nuys High School, was twenty-
two years old and wore his hair in a sharp 1951
ducktail, which perhaps suggests the extent to
which he, like everyone else in the room, heard
a different drummer. "I didn't lose no fortune,"
he said, "but I lost all the money I could get my

hands on, it began in the Marine Corps, I met a lot of pigeons in Vietnam, I was making easy money and it was, you might say, this period in my life that, uh, led to my downfall."

The smoke grew thicker, the testimony more intense. I had not heard so many revelations of a certain kind since I used to fall into conversations on Greyhound buses under the misapprehension that it was a good way to learn about life. "See, I had just got through embezzling a large sum of money from my employer," they were saying to one another, and "I started out for a Canoga Park meeting and turned around on the freeway, that was last Wednesday. I ended up in Gardena and now I'm on the verge of divorce again." *Mea culpa,* they appeared to be crying, and many of them had cried it the night before and the night before that: every night there is a Gamblers Anonymous meeting somewhere around Los Angeles, somewhere like Long Beach or Canoga Park or Downey or Culver City, and the ideal is to attend five or six a week. "I never made this Gardena meeting before," someone explained, "for one simple reason only, which is I break out in a cold sweat every time I pass Gardena on the freeway even, but I'm here tonight because every night I make a meeting is a night I don't place a bet, which with the help of God and you people is 1,223 nights now."

There were certain curiosities in the way they talked to one another. As if they were casters of horoscopes (and perhaps some of them were), they kept fanatical track not only of their own but of everyone else's important "dates" ("December third, '65, that was a bad date for me because that was the night I wrote the first phony check in the amount of $343, but it was an important date for Frank L., that date one year later made eight months on the same job for Frank L., even though he subsequently lost it, which shows that some of us are struggling on the same date when others of us are slipping, which is the miracle of G.A."); they spoke in general as if from some subverbal swamp, snatching at phrases as they floated by. "Now that I'm on the program I have the togetherness with my family," someone said, and "the most important thing I've gotten out of the program at the present time is my, uh, mental thinking." "As you all know I reached my bottom that night of

November twenty-eighth over at the Normandie Club," another said, "and after that I got serenity." "That's my ideal," someone added. "Getting serenity."

There was nothing particularly wrong with any of it, and yet there was something not quite right, something troubling. At first I thought that it was simply the predilection of many of the members to dwell upon how "powerless" they were, how buffeted by forces beyond their control. There was a great deal of talk about miracles, and Higher Presences, and a Power Greater Than Ourselves; the Gamblers Anonymous program, like that of Alcoholics Anonymous, tends to reinforce the addict's own rather passive view of his situation. (The first of the G.A. "Twelve Steps" involves admitting that one's life "has become" unmanageable. Five steps further, and still being acted upon, one avers that one is ready to "have these defects of character removed.") "My neighbor introduced me to Hollywood Park, big favor he did me," someone said that night. "They oughta bomb this Gardena," a young man whispered to me fervently. "A kid goes in one of those places, he's hooked for life."

But of course, *mea culpa* always turns out to be not entirely *mea.* Still, there was coffee to be drunk, a cake to be cut: it was Frank L.'s "birthday" in Gamblers Anonymous. After six years on the program he had finally completed a full year without placing a bet, and was being honored with a one-year pin ("Frank L., I want you to remember just one thing, the one-year pin is just a leafmark, just a bookmark in the book of life") and a cake, a white cake with an inscription in pink icing: MIRACLES STILL HAPPEN, the cake read. "It hasn't been easy," Frank L. said, surrounded by his wife, his children, and his wife's parents. "But in the last three, four weeks we've gotten a . . . a *serenity* at home." Well, there it was. I got out fast then, before anyone could say "serenity" again, for it is a word I associate with death, and for several days after that meeting I wanted only to be in places where the lights were bright and no one counted days.

1968

A Trip to Xanadu

It has been for almost half a century a peculiar and affecting image in the California mind: San Simeon, *"La Cuesta Encantada,"* the phantasmagoric barony that William Randolph Hearst made for himself on the sunburned hills above the San Luis Obispo County coast. California children used to hear about San Simeon when they were very small (I know because I was one of them), used to be told to watch for it from Highway 1, quite far in the distance, crested on the hill, the great Moorish towers and battlements shimmering in the sun or floating fantastically just above the coastal fog; San Simeon was a place which, once seen from the highway, was ever in the mind, a material fact which existed in proof of certain abstract principles. San Simeon seemed to con-

firm the boundless promise of the place we lived.
The gates were always barred on that road up the
hill, and yet there was a kind of frontier accessi-
bility about the Hearsts; the Hearst money was
Western money, money that had come originally
from a silver strike in Nevada, money made and
spent in a singularly Western spirit of luck, imagination, irresponsibility, and general flamboyance.
If a Hearst could build himself a castle, then every
man could be a king.

San Simeon was, moreover, exactly the castle
a child would build, if a child had $220 million
and could spend $40 million of it on a castle: a
sand castle, an implausibility, a place swimming
in warm golden light and theatrical mists, a plea-
sure dome decreed by a man who insisted, out of
the one dark fear we all know about, that all the
surfaces be gay and brilliant and playful. More
than any other place ever built in this country,
San Simeon was dedicated to the proposition
that all the pleasures of infinity are to be found
in the here and the now. The leaves never fell at
San Simeon, nothing went bare or died. All year
long the roses and fuchsia and the bougainvillea

blossomed, half a million gallons of water glittered in the great pools, zebras and eland roamed the golden hills. The carillon bells could be heard for thirty miles. Brilliant Sienese flags fluttered over the long refectory dining tables. The guests ate pressed duck and wiped their hands on paper napkins: again, a child's fantasy, every meal a picnic. The spirit of San Simeon was uninhibited by nervous adult distinctions about what was correct and what was not, what was good and what was less good, what was "art" and what not: if William Randolph Hearst liked something he bought it, and brought it to San Simeon. And a child would people his castle with exactly the same cast: there was the omnipotent King, the spurned Queen, the captive Princess from another land. There were the ambitious underlings, bearing dispatches from the capitals of the earth. And of course there were the courtiers, the decorative courtiers, some of whom came for the weekend and stayed for months, because no one was banished from this court unless he drank too much, or mentioned death. There were to be no shadows at all in this fairy tale: San Simeon was to be the kingdom where nobody dies.

And there it all was, floating on the hill for any child to see. I actually saw it there only three or four times, but I heard about it, and I remembered it, and San Simeon was an imaginative idea that affected me, shaped my own imagination in the way that all children are shaped by the actual and emotional geography of the place in which they grow up, by the stories they are told and the stories they invent. Because that was so, I made a trip not long ago to San Simeon, which since 1958 has been a state monument (the King did die, of course, in 1951, and his sons gave the castle to the state). I joined one of the daily tours through certain of the 147 rooms in the Great House and the guest houses.

It was what I had expected, and it was not. In most ways, most of the physical ways, San Simeon now looks precisely as it was supposed to have looked when William Randolph Hearst was alive: the ranch has dwindled from 275,000 to 85,000 acres, but it remains a working cattle ranch, and 85,000 acres is still pretty much as far as one can see from the broad tiled terraces. The private zoo is gone, the gnu and the sloth bears and the elephant, but a few zebras still graze in

the stands of bay laurel on the hill. The art histo-
rians who visit the place now and then complain
that the tapestries are fading, the paintings crack-
ing and the polychrome wooden statuary flaking,
the carved wooden ceilings being destroyed by
insects; except for such incursions of time, however, and except for the absence of cut flowers, the
state maintains the houses just as Hearst last saw
them. The roses still blossom outside, and the sun
glistens on the palm fronds, and the yellow hills
running down to the sea absorb the light in that
way peculiar to the California countryside. Nothing seems to have changed, and yet everything
has, for in a way the state has made San Simeon
what it never was, just another rich man's estate.
The visitors come, as many as four million a year,
in slacks and straw hats and hair rollers; they pay
their three dollars and walk through on strips of
protective nylon carpeting. They advise one another on snapshot angles, and speculate about
how much it costs to heat the place. In the peak
seasons the state hires eighty-nine civil-service
guides and tour aides; some of them live in the
servants' quarters, all of them swim in the Nep-

tune Pool between six and eight each evening. They have barbecues on the terraces, and after-hours discussion groups, with such topics as "The Generation Gap." The guides wear khaki uniforms and are treasuries of fact: *2,144 rose bushes in Mr. Hearst's gardens, 5,400 volumes in Mr. Hearst's private library, at one time Mr. Hearst was noted for buying up one quarter of the world's art objects, in 504 categories of art.* "If you'd been a guest of Mr. Hearst's . . . ," they say, over and over again. If you'd been a guest of Mr. Hearst's, you could have played the Wurlitzer baby grand before dinner. If you'd been a guest of Mr. Hearst's, you could have seen a movie after dinner, *and actually sat next to the cast of the movie in the projection room.* It is a reverence which extends unto the Hearst sons, who occasionally stay at San Simeon, in a twenty-room guest house reserved for their use. "If you saw them, you probably wouldn't recognize them," the guide advises, "because they wouldn't be dressed any differently from you." I listened to the guides for a long while, and had a hard time getting the tone. And then I recognized it: it was a tone reflecting the idolatry of the rich that so often accompanies the democratization of things, the flattening out. I had taken a child up there with me, a niece from Connecticut who had never before heard of San Simeon, and she liked the flowers and the pools and the ornate ceilings, but it occurred to me as we left that she would have found it more affecting had she only glimpsed it from Highway 1, the gates barred, the castle floating in the distance. Make a place available to the eyes, and in certain ways it is no longer available to the imagination.

1968

On Being Unchosen
by the College of One's Choice

Dear Joan," the letter begins, although the writer
did not know me at all. The letter is dated April 25,
1952, and for a long time now it has been in a
drawer in my mother's house, the kind of back-
bedroom drawer given over to class prophecies
and dried butterfly orchids and newspaper photographs that show eight bridesmaids and two
flower girls inspecting a sixpence in a bride's shoe.
What slight emotional investment I ever had in
dried butterfly orchids and pictures of myself as
a bridesmaid has proved evanescent, but I still
have an investment in the letter, which, except for
the "Dear Joan," is mimeographed. I got the letter
out as an object lesson for a seventeen-year-old
cousin who is unable to eat or sleep as she waits to
hear from what she keeps calling the colleges of
her choice. Here is what the letter says:

The Committee on Admissions asks me to
inform you that it is unable to take favorable
action upon your application for admission
to Stanford University. While you have met
the minimum requirements, we regret that
because of the severity of the competition,
the Committee cannot include you in the
group to be admitted. The Committee joins
me in extending you every good wish for the
successful continuation of your education.
Sincerely yours, Rixford K. Snyder, Director
of Admissions.

I remember quite clearly the afternoon I
opened that letter. I stood reading and reread-
ing it, my sweater and my books fallen on the
hall floor, trying to interpret the words in some
less final way, the phrases "unable to take" and
"favorable action" fading in and out of focus until
the sentence made no sense at all. We lived then
in a big dark Victorian house, and I had a sharp
and dolorous image of myself growing old in it,
never going to school anywhere, the spinster in
Washington Square. I went upstairs to my room

and locked the door and for a couple of hours I cried. For a while I sat on the floor of my closet and buried my face in an old quilted robe and later, after the situation's real humiliations (all my friends who applied to Stanford had been admitted) had faded into safe theatrics, I sat on the edge of the bathtub and thought about swallowing the contents of an old bottle of codeine-and-Empirin. I saw myself in an oxygen tent, with Rixford K. Snyder hovering outside, although how the news was to reach Rixford K. Snyder was a plot point that troubled me even as I counted out the tablets.

Of course I did not take the tablets. I spent the rest of the spring in sullen but mild rebellion, sitting around drive-ins, listening to Tulsa evangelists on the car radio, and in the summer I fell in love with someone who wanted to be a golf pro, and I spent a lot of time watching him practice putting, and in the fall I went to a junior college a couple of hours a day and made up the credits I needed to go to the University of California at Berkeley. The next year a friend at Stanford asked me to write him a paper on Conrad's *Nostromo,* and I did, and he got an A on it. I got a B- on the

same paper at Berkeley, and the specter of Rixford K. Snyder was exorcised.

So it worked out all right, my single experience
in that most conventional middle-class confron-
tation, the child vs. the Admissions Committee.
But that was in the benign world of country California in 1952, and I think it must be more difficult for children I know now, children whose
lives from the age of two or three are a series of
perilously programmed steps, each of which must
be successfully negotiated in order to avoid just
such a letter as mine from one or another of the
Rixford K. Snyders of the world. An acquaintance
told me recently that there were ninety applicants
for the seven openings in the kindergarten of an
expensive school in which she hoped to enroll her
four-year-old, and that she was frantic because
none of the four-year-old's letters of recommen-
dation had mentioned the child's "interest in art."
Had I been raised under that pressure, I suspect
I would have taken the codeine-and-Empirin on
that April afternoon in 1952. My rejection was different, my humiliation private: no parental hopes
rode on whether I was admitted to Stanford, or

anywhere. Of course my mother and father wanted
me to be happy, and of course they expected that
happiness would necessarily entail accomplishment, but the terms of that accomplishment were
my affair. Their idea of their own and of my worth
remained independent of where, or even if, I went
to college. Our social situation was static, and the
question of "right" schools, so traditionally urgent
to the upwardly mobile, did not arise. When my
father was told that I had been rejected by Stanford, he shrugged and offered me a drink.

I think about that shrug with a great deal of
appreciation whenever I hear parents talking
about their children's "chances." What makes me
uneasy is the sense that they are merging their
children's chances with their own, demanding of
a child that he make good not only for himself but
for the greater glory of his father and mother. Of
course it is harder to get into college now than it
once was. Of course there are more children than
"desirable" openings. But we are deluding ourselves if we pretend that desirable schools ben-
efit the child alone. ("I wouldn't care at all about
his getting into Yale if it weren't for Vietnam," a

father told me not long ago, quite unconscious of his own speciousness; it would have been malicious of me to suggest that one could also get a deferment at Long Beach State.) Getting into college has become an ugly business, malignant in its consumption and diversion of time and energy and true interests, and not its least deleterious aspect is how the children themselves accept it. They talk casually and unattractively of their "first, second, and third choices," of how their "first-choice" application (to Stephens, say) does not actually reflect their first choice (their first choice was Smith, but their adviser said their chances were low, so why "waste" the application?); they are calculating about the expectation of rejections, about their "backup" possibilities, about getting the right sport and the right extracurricular activities to "balance" the application, about juggling confirmations when their third choice accepts before their first choice answers. They are wise in the white lie here, the small self-aggrandizement there, in the importance of letters from "names" their parents scarcely know. I have heard conversations among sixteen-year-

olds who were exceeded in their skill at manipu-
lative self-promotion only by applicants for large
literary grants.

And of course none of it matters very much
at all, none of these early successes, early fail-
ures. I wonder if we had better not find some
way to let our children know this, some way to
extricate our expectations from theirs, some way
to let them work through their own rejections
and sullen rebellions and interludes with golf
pros, unassisted by anxious prompting from the
wings. Finding one's role at seventeen is problem
enough, without being handed somebody else's
script.

1968

Pretty Nancy

Pretty Nancy Reagan, the wife of the governor of California, was standing in the dining room of her rented house on Forty-fifth Street in Sacramento listening to a television newsman explain what he wanted to do. She was listening attentively. Nancy Reagan is a very attentive listener. The television crew wanted to watch her, the newsman said, while she was doing precisely what she would ordinarily be doing on a Tuesday morning at home. Since I was also there to watch her doing precisely what she would ordinarily be doing on a Tuesday morning at home, we seemed to be on the verge of exploring certain media frontiers: the television newsman and the two cameramen could watch Nancy Reagan being watched by me, or I could watch Nancy Reagan being watched by the three of them, or one of the cameramen could step back and do a *cinéma vérité* study of the rest of us all watching and being watched by one another. I had the distinct sense that we were on the track of something revelatory, the truth about Nancy Reagan at twenty-four frames a second, but the television newsman opted to overlook the moment's peculiar essence. He suggested that we watch Nancy Reagan picking some flowers in the garden. "That's something you might ordinarily do, isn't it?" he asked. "Indeed it is," Nancy Reagan said with spirit. Nancy Reagan says almost everything with spirit, perhaps because she was an actress for a couple of years and has the beginning actress's habit of investing even the most casual lines with a good deal more dramatic emphasis than is ordinarily called for on a Tuesday morning on Forty-fifth Street in Sacramento.

"Actually," she added then, with the air of someone about to disclose a delightful surprise, "actually, I really *do* need flowers."

She smiled at each of us, and I smiled back. We had all been smiling quite a bit that morning. "And then," the television newsman said thoughtfully, surveying the dining room table, "even though you've got a beautiful arrangement right now, we could set up the pretense of your arranging, you know, the flowers."

We all smiled at one another again, and then Nancy Reagan walked resolutely into the garden, equipped with a decorative straw basket about six inches in diameter. "Uh, Mrs. Reagan," the newsman called after her. "May I ask what you're going to select for flowers?"

"Why, I don't know," she said, pausing with her basket on a garden step. The scene was evolving its own choreography.

"Do you think you could use rhododendrons?"

Nancy Reagan looked critically at a rhododendron bush. Then she turned to the newsman and smiled. "Did you know there's a Nancy Reagan rose now?"

"Uh, no," he said. "I didn't."

"It's awfully pretty, it's kind of, oh, a kind of coral color."

"Would the . . . the Nancy Reagan rose be something you might be likely to pick now?"

A silvery peal of laughter. "I could certainly

pick it. But I won't be *using* it." A pause. "I *can* use the rhododendron."

"Fine," the newsman said. "Just fine. Now I'll ask a question, and if you could just be nipping a bud as you answer it..."

"Nipping a bud," Nancy Reagan repeated, taking her place in front of the rhododendron bush.

"Let's have a dry run," a cameraman said.

The newsman looked at him. "In other words, by a dry run, you mean you want her to fake nipping the bud."

"Fake the nip, yeah," the cameraman said. "Fake the nip."

I tell you about all that because whenever I think of Nancy Reagan now I think of her just so, the frame frozen, pretty Nancy Reagan about to pluck a rhododendron blossom too large to fit into her decorative six-inch basket. Nancy Reagan has an interested smile, the smile of a good wife, a good mother, a good hostess, the smile of someone who grew up in comfort and went to Smith College and has a father who is a distinguished neurosurgeon (her father's entry in the 1966–67 *Who's Who* runs nine lines longer than her hus-

band's) and a husband who is the definition of
Nice Guy, not to mention governor of California,
the smile of a woman who seems to be playing out
some middle-class American woman's daydream,
circa 1948. The set for this daydream is perfectly
dressed, every detail correct. There in the rental
house on Forty-fifth Street the white matchbooks
read EXECUTIVE MANSION, but it is not hard to imagine them reading NANCY AND RONNIE, and there on
the coffee table in the living room lie precisely the
right magazines for the life being portrayed: *Town
& Country, Vogue, Time, Life, Newsweek, Sports
Illustrated, Fortune, ARTnews*. There are two
dogs, named Lady and Fuzzy, and there are two
children, named Pattie and Ronnie. Pattie, fifteen,
is described as artistic, and she goes to a boarding
school in Arizona. Ronnie, ten, is referred to as a
regular boy, and he goes to a private school in Sacramento. He is also referred to as "the Skipper."
Everyone on the set smiles, the social secretary,
the state guard, the cook, the gardeners. And, out
there in the garden, Nancy Reagan smiles, about
to pluck the rhododendron blossom. "Oh, no, no,
no," she is saying to the television newsman, who

seems to have asked his question. "There's been no difference at all as far as our friends are concerned." She studies her basket. "If there was a difference, why, they just wouldn't be friends. Your friends are . . . your *friends*."

It is later the same day. Nancy Reagan has plucked and arranged the rhododendron blossoms several times, and the television crew has gone. Nancy Reagan has shown me the game room, where the governor and the Skipper and some of the state legislators like to play with electric trains. She has shown me the original drawings for some *Peanuts* cartoon strips, which Charles Schulz gave to the governor after the governor declared a Happiness-Is-Having-Charles-Schulz-as-a-California-Resident Day. She has shown me a photograph of the governor jumping a horse. ("His horse Nancy D," she mused, "who died the day we came to Sacramento.") She has told me that the governor never wore makeup even in motion pictures, and that politics is rougher than the picture business because you do not have the studio to protect you. We have gone downtown, and she has shown me how she replaced the old padded leather walls in the State Capitol ("dark, horrible, shabby") with beige burlap and carpeted the floors in a pleasing shade of green. "Having a pretty place to work is important to a man," she has advised me. She has shown me the apothecary jar of hard candies she keeps filled on the governor's desk. She has shown me how she says hello to Girl Scouts when she comes across them in the Capitol corridors.

She has shown me all those things, and now we are back in the living room of the rented house on Forty-fifth Street, waiting for the Skipper to come home from school. The Skipper's arrival is, I have been told, the pivotal point of Nancy Reagan's day.

The Skipper is expected at 3:20. He goes to a private school and comes home in a car pool. On this day Ronald Azavedo, a State Highway Patrol officer assigned to the Reagans, is driving the car in the pool. We wait awhile longer, but don't hear the car drive up. Nancy Reagan goes to the stairway and listens a moment. "I believe he slipped up the back stairway," she says. "Ronnie? Ronnie?"

Ronnie does not seem to be planning an appearance. "Bye," he says from somewhere.

"Come in for just a minute, Ronnie."

"Lo," he says, appearing in the doorway.

"How's Chuck's cold?" Nancy Reagan asks.

"Chuck doesn't have a cold."

"Chuck doesn't have a cold?"

"No. Bruce has braces."

"Bruce has braces," Nancy Reagan repeats.

"Bye," the Skipper says.

"Bye," I say.

Nancy Reagan smiles radiantly at me, and calls Ronald Azavedo to drive me back downtown. "I don't believe in being an absentee mother," she says to me. "I just don't."

1968

Fathers, Sons, Screaming Eagles

I hope you don't think I'm a hippie," said the man to whom I was talking in the Crown Room of the Stardust Hotel on the Las Vegas Strip in Las Vegas, Nevada. "I'm just kind of, you know, growing this beard." His name tag said Skip Skivington. He was probably in his early forties and he had been at Bastogne with the 101st Airborne Division in 1944 and his voice was gentle and apologetic and I had not thought him a hippie. It was the first evening of the 101st Airborne Association's twenty-third annual reunion, one weekend in Las Vegas not long ago. Outside the late-summer sky burned all day and all night and inside it was perpetually cold and carpeted and no perceptible time of day or night, and here, in the Crown Room of the Stardust, along with a great many wives and

a few children, were a couple of hundred survivors of Normandy, Bastogne, the Battle of the
Bulge. I had come over from Los Angeles to find
them and knew that I had found them when I
walked into the Stardust bar and saw a couple of
men in sport shirts and overseas caps. "Just wait
a minute," one of them had been saying. "I gotta
finish this brew." In the afternoon they had com-
mandeered the Stardust swimming pool for a
beer party, and now they were lining up for a buf-
fet dinner (roast beef, ham, coleslaw, sliced beets,
sliced tomatoes, American cheese, and dinner
rolls), filling plates and finding tables and snapping the toy metal crickets that had been the 101st's
identification code on D-day. "General McAuliffe.
General," called a weathered man in an overseas
cap as he threaded his way through the tables with
a small child, two or three years old, by the hand.
"Look at the boy. I wanted to show you the boy."

Almost everyone else had found friends and a
table by then, but Skip Skivington still stood with
me. He was telling me about his son. His son, he
said, had been missing in Vietnam since Mother's
Day. I did not know what to say, but because Skip

Skivington was active in the 101st Airborne Association, I asked if his son had belonged to the 101st.
The father looked at me and then away. "I talked
him out of it," he said finally. He reached into his
coat pocket then and brought out a newspaper
clipping, preserved in clear plastic, a story about
his son: where he had gone to high school, the
report that he was missing, the action in which
he had last been seen. There was a snapshot of
the boy, his face indistinct in the engraving dots,
a blond eighteen-year-old sitting on a rock and
smiling. I gave the clipping back to Skip Skivington, and before he put it in his pocket again he
looked at it a long while, smoothed out an imagined crease, and studied the fragment of news-
print as if it held some answer.

   The indistinct face of the boy and the distinct
face of the father stayed in my mind all that evening, all that weekend, and perhaps it was their
faces that made those few days in Las Vegas seem
so charged with unspoken questions, ambiguities
only dimly perceived. In most ways the reunion
was a happy occasion. The wives had pretty
dresses, and everyone liked Las Vegas, agreed that

it was definitely the place for the reunion ("I've
been to every reunion and I never saw so many
guys as right here in Vegas, Vegas is definitely
the place to have it"), agreed that the Stardust's
Lido Revue was—well, bare breasts are risqué,
but the girls were just lovely and the whole thing
was tastefully done, especially the ice-skating
sequence, which was a work of art. There were
meetings to be held, Gold Star Mothers, like Mrs.
C. J. (Mom) Miller, to be recognized. There was a
new president of the association to be installed.
"Thanks, Bernie, fellow Screaming Eagles," said
the new president, "men of the 101st, our wives,
our friends, our Gold Star Mothers . . ."

There was a wives' luncheon, a hospitality suite.
"I'll be floatin' around the hotel in the afternoon.
I'm not gonna *touch* that hospitality suite till after
two," said someone to whom I was talking. There
were Army movies, and I sat with a sprinkling
of wives in the cool darkness and learned about
the future of the Weapons Command, the function of Procurement. The wives slipped off their
shoes and consulted slips of paper. "Not counting
a couple of quarters at the airport," one of them

said, "we were down twenty-seven dollars yesterday and up twelve dollars today. That's not bad,
that's *net.*" There were telegrams to be sent, to the
101st in Vietnam ("Keep that Eagle Screaming"),
and telegrams to be read, from Hubert Humphrey
("We are not a nation that has lost its way, but a
nation seeking a better way"). There was even a
Teen Room, where a handful of children sat on
folding chairs and regarded a Wurlitzer in sullen
ennui.

And of course there were speeches. Maxwell
Taylor came, to point out similarities between
the Battle of the Bulge and the Tet Offensive. "By
the way these things were reported, many of the
people at home had the impression that we were
losing the Bulge, just as they now have the impression that . . ." A colonel from Vietnam came, flown
in to assure the guests that operations there were
characterized by high *esprit,* rugged determina-
tion, that "the men in Vietnam are exactly like you
were, and I was, twenty, twenty-five years ago."
Gen. Anthony McAuliffe came, the man who said
"Nuts" when the Germans asked for a surrender
at Bastogne, and he said that he would be with the

group in Holland next year to commemorate the twenty-fifth anniversary of the European invasion. "We'll visit our Dutch friends," he said, "and revive memories of that great adventure we had there."

And of course there it was, that was it. They had indeed had a great adventure, an essential adventure, and almost everyone in the room had been nineteen and twenty years old when they had it, and they had survived and come home and their wives had given birth to sons, and now those sons were nineteen, twenty, and perhaps it was not such a great adventure this time. Perhaps it was hard to bring quite the same urgency to holding a position in a Vietnamese village or two that they had brought to liberating Europe. On the night of the speeches I sat with a man named Walter Davis and his wife, a soft-faced woman in a good black dress. Walter Davis jumped into Holland in 1944, and now he works for the Metropolitan Life in Lawndale, California, and has three children, a daughter of eighteen, a son of fourteen, and a daughter of three. There was a Dutch girl at the table, and Mrs. Davis asked her to write a message in Dutch to their son. "Eddie's at that age where he's interested in everything his father did when he was a teenager, everything about the war and Holland," Mrs. Davis said. We talked awhile, and I mentioned, because those faces were very much with me, that I had met someone whose son was missing in Vietnam. Walter Davis said nothing for a moment. "I never thought of dying then," he said suddenly, after a while. "I see it a little differently now. I didn't look at it from the parents' point of view then. I was eighteen, nineteen. I wanted to go, couldn't stand not to go. I got to see Paris, Berlin, got to see places I'd heard about but never dreamed I'd see. Now I've got a boy, well, in four years maybe he'll have to go." Walter Davis broke open a roll, buttered it carefully, and put it down again, untouched. "I see it a little differently now," he said.

1968

Why I Write

Of course I stole the title for this talk, from George Orwell. One reason I stole it was that I like the sound of the words: Why I Write. There you have three short unambiguous words that share a sound, and the sound they share is this:

I

I

I

In many ways, writing is the act of saying I, of imposing oneself upon other people, of saying *listen to me, see it my way, change your mind.* It's an aggressive, even a hostile act. You can disguise its aggressiveness all you want with veils of subordinate clauses and qualifiers and tentative subjunctives, with ellipses and evasions—with the whole manner of intimating rather than claiming, of

alluding rather than stating—but there's no getting around the fact that setting words on paper is
the tactic of a secret bully, an invasion, an imposition of the writer's sensibility on the reader's most
private space.

I stole the title not only because the words
sounded right but because they seemed to sum
up, in a no-nonsense way, all I have to tell you.
Like many writers I have only this one "subject,"
this one "area": the act of writing. I can bring
you no reports from any other front. I may have
other interests: I am "interested," for example, in
marine biology, but I don't flatter myself that you
would come out to hear me talk about it. I am not
a scholar. I am not in the least an intellectual,
which is not to say that when I hear the word
"intellectual" I reach for my gun, but only to say
that I do not think in abstracts. During the years
when I was an undergraduate at Berkeley I tried,
with a kind of hopeless late-adolescent energy, to
buy some temporary visa into the world of ideas,
to forge for myself a mind that could deal with the
abstract.

In short I tried to think. I failed. My attention

veered inexorably back to the specific, to the tangible, to what was generally considered, by everyone I knew then and for that matter have known since, the peripheral. I would try to contemplate the Hegelian dialectic and would find myself concentrating instead on a flowering pear tree outside my window and the particular way the petals fell on my floor. I would try to read linguistic theory and would find myself wondering instead if the lights were on in the Bevatron up the hill. When I say that I was wondering if the lights were on in the Bevatron you might immediately suspect, if you deal in ideas at all, that I was registering the Bevatron as a political symbol, thinking in shorthand about the military-industrial complex and its role in the university community, but you would be wrong. I was only wondering if the lights were on in the Bevatron, and how they looked. A physical fact.

I had trouble graduating from Berkeley, not because of this inability to deal with ideas— I was majoring in English, and I could locate the house-and-garden imagery in *The Portrait of a Lady* as well as the next person, "imagery" being

by definition the kind of specific that got my
attention—but simply because I had neglected
to take a course in Milton. For reasons which now
sound baroque I needed a degree by the end of
that summer, and the English department finally
agreed, if I would come down from Sacramento
every Friday and talk about the cosmology of
Paradise Lost, to certify me proficient in Milton.
I did this. Some Fridays I took the Greyhound
bus, other Fridays I caught the Southern Pacific's
City of San Francisco on the last leg of its trans-
continental trip. I can no longer tell you whether
Milton put the sun or the earth at the center of his
universe in *Paradise Lost,* the central question
of at least one century and a topic about which I
wrote ten thousand words that summer, but I can
still recall the exact rancidity of the butter in the
City of San Francisco's dining car, and the way the
tinted windows on the Greyhound bus cast the oil
refineries around Carquinez Strait into a grayed
and obscurely sinister light. In short my attention
was always on the periphery, on what I could see
and taste and touch, on the butter, and the Greyhound bus. During those years I was traveling on

what I knew to be a very shaky passport, forged papers: I knew that I was no legitimate resident in any world of ideas. I knew I couldn't think. All I knew then was what I couldn't do. All I knew then was what I wasn't, and it took me some years to discover what I was.

Which was a writer.

By which I mean not a "good" writer or a "bad" writer but simply a writer, a person whose most absorbed and passionate hours are spent arranging words on pieces of paper. Had my credentials been in order I would never have become a writer. Had I been blessed with even limited access to my own mind there would have been no reason to write. I write entirely to find out what I'm thinking, what I'm looking at, what I see and what it means. What I want and what I fear. Why did the oil refineries around Carquinez Strait seem sinister to me in the summer of 1956? Why have the night lights in the Bevatron burned in my mind for twenty years? *What is going on in these pictures in my mind?*

When I talk about pictures in my mind I am talking, quite specifically, about images that shimmer around the edges. There used to be an illustration in every elementary psychology book showing a cat drawn by a patient in varying stages of schizophrenia. This cat had a shimmer around it. You could see the molecular structure breaking down at the very edges of the cat: the cat became the background and the background the cat, everything interacting, exchanging ions. People on hallucinogens describe the same perception of objects. I'm not a schizophrenic, nor do I take hallucinogens, but certain images do shimmer for me. Look hard enough, and you can't miss the shimmer. It's there. You can't think too much about these pictures that shimmer. You just lie low and let them develop. You stay quiet. You don't talk to many people and you keep your nervous system from shorting out and you try to locate the cat in the shimmer, the grammar in the picture.

Just as I meant "shimmer" literally I mean "grammar" literally. Grammar is a piano I play by ear, since I seem to have been out of school the year the rules were mentioned. All I know about grammar is its infinite power. To shift the structure of a sentence alters the meaning of that sentence, as definitely and inflexibly as the position of a camera alters the meaning of the object photographed. Many people know about camera angles now, but not so many know about sentences. The arrangement of the words matters, and the arrangement you want can be found in the picture in your mind. The picture dictates the arrangement. The picture dictates whether this will be a sentence with or without clauses, a sentence that ends hard or a dying-fall sentence, long or short, active or passive. The picture tells you how to arrange the words and the arrangement of the words tells you, or tells me, what's going on in the picture. *Nota bene:*

It tells you.

You don't tell it.

Let me show you what I mean by pictures in the mind. I began *Play It as It Lays* just as I have begun each of my novels, with no notion of "character" or "plot" or even "incident." I had only two pictures in my mind, more about which later, and a technical intention, which was to write a novel so elliptical and fast that it would be over before you noticed it, a novel so fast that it would scarcely exist on the page at all. About the pictures: the first was of white space. Empty space. This was clearly

the picture that dictated the narrative intention
of the book—a book in which anything that happened would happen off the page, a "white" book
to which the reader would have to bring his or
her own bad dreams—and yet this picture told
me no "story," suggested no situation. The second
picture did. This second picture was of something
actually witnessed. A young woman with long
hair and a short white halter dress walks through
the casino at the Riviera in Las Vegas at one in the
morning. She crosses the casino alone and picks
up a house telephone. I watch her because I have
heard her paged, and recognize her name: she is a
minor actress I see around Los Angeles from time
to time, in places like Jax and once in a gynecolo-
gist's office in the Beverly Hills Clinic, but have
never met. I know nothing about her. Who is pag-
ing her? Why is she here to be paged? How exactly
did she come to this? It was precisely this moment
in Las Vegas that made *Play It as It Lays* begin to
tell itself to me, but the moment appears in the
novel only obliquely, in a chapter which begins:

Maria made a list of things she would never
do. She would never: walk through the

Sands or Caesar's alone after midnight. She
would never: ball at a party, do S-M unless
she wanted to, borrow furs from Abe Lipsey,
deal. She would never: carry a Yorkshire in
Beverly Hills.

That is the beginning of the chapter and that
is also the end of the chapter, which may suggest
what I meant by "white space."

I recall having a number of pictures in my mind
when I began the novel I just finished, *A Book
of Common Prayer*. As a matter of fact one of
these pictures was of that Bevatron I mentioned,
although I would be hard put to tell you a story
in which nuclear energy figures. Another was a
newspaper photograph of a hijacked 707 burning on the desert in the Middle East. Another was
the night view from a room in which I once spent
a week with paratyphoid, a hotel room on the
Colombian coast. My husband and I seemed to be
on the Colombian coast representing the United
States of America at a film festival (I recall invok-
ing the name Jack Valenti a lot, as if its reitera-
tion could make me well), and it was a bad place
to have fever, not only because my indisposition

offended our hosts but because every night in this hotel the generator failed. The lights went out. The elevator stopped. My husband would go to the event of the evening and make excuses for me and I would stay alone in this hotel room, in the dark. I remember standing at the window trying to call Bogotá (the telephone seemed to work on the same principle as the generator) and watching the night wind come up and wondering what I was doing eleven degrees off the equator with a fever of 103. The view from that window definitely figures in *A Book of Common Prayer,* as does the burning 707, and yet none of these pictures told me the story I needed.

The picture that did, the picture that shimmered and made these other images coalesce, was of the Panama airport at 6:00 a.m. I was in this airport only once, on a plane to Bogotá that stopped for an hour to refuel, but the way it looked that morning remained superimposed on everything I saw until the day I finished *A Book of Common Prayer*. I lived in that airport for several years. I can still feel the hot air when I step off the plane, can see the heat already rising off the tarmac at

6:00 a.m. I can feel the skirt damp and wrinkled on my legs. I can feel the asphalt stick to my sandals. I remember the big tail of a Pan American plane floating motionless down at the end of the tarmac. I remember the sound of a slot machine in the waiting room. I could tell you that I remember a particular woman in the airport, an American woman, a *norteamericana,* a thin *norteamericana* about forty who wore a big square emerald in lieu of a wedding ring, but there was no such woman there.

I put this woman in the airport later. I made this woman up, just as I later made up a country to put the airport in, and a family to run the country. This woman in the airport is neither catching a plane nor meeting one. She is ordering tea in the airport coffee shop. In fact she is not simply "ordering" tea but insisting that the water be boiled, in front of her, for twenty minutes. Why is this woman in this airport? Why is she going nowhere, where has she been? Where did she get that big emerald? What derangement, or disassociation, makes her believe that her will to see the water boiled can possibly prevail?

She had been going to one airport or another
for four months, one could see it, looking
at the visas on her passport. All those airports where Charlotte Douglas's passport
had been stamped would have looked alike.
Sometimes the sign on the tower would say
"BIENVENIDOS" and sometimes the sign on the
tower would say "BIENVENUE," some places
were wet and hot and others were dry and
hot, but at each of these airports the pastel
concrete walls would rust and stain and the
swamp off the runway would be littered
with the fuselages of cannibalized Fairchild
F-227s and the water would need boiling.

I knew why Charlotte went to the airport
even if Victor did not.

I knew about airports.

These lines appear about halfway through *A
Book of Common Prayer,* but I wrote them during the second week I worked on the book, long
before I had any idea where Charlotte Douglas
had been or why she went to airports. Until I
wrote these lines I had no character called Victor

in mind: the necessity for mentioning a name, and the name Victor, occurred to me as I wrote the sentence. *I knew why Charlotte went to the airport* sounded incomplete. *I knew why Charlotte went to the airport even if Victor did not* carried a little more narrative drive. Most important of all, until I wrote these lines I did not know who "I" was, who was telling the story. I had intended until that moment that the "I" be no more than the voice of the author, a nineteenth-century omniscient narrator. But there it was:

"I knew why Charlotte went to the airport even if Victor did not."

"I knew about airports."

This "I" was the voice of no author in my house. This "I" was someone who not only knew why Charlotte went to the airport but also knew someone called Victor. Who was Victor? Who was this narrator? Why was this narrator telling me this story? Let me tell you one thing about why writers write: had I known the answer to any of these questions I would never have needed to write a novel.

1976

Telling Stories

In the fall of 1954, when I was nineteen and a junior at Berkeley, I was one of perhaps a dozen students admitted to the late Mark Schorer's English 106A, a kind of "writers' workshop" which met for discussion three hours a week and required that each student produce, over the course of the semester, at least five short stories. No auditors were allowed. Voices were kept low. English 106A was widely regarded in the fall of 1954 as a kind of sacramental experience, an initiation into the grave world of real writers, and I remember each meeting of this class as an occasion of acute excitement and dread. I remember each other member of this class as older and wiser than I had hope of ever being (it had not yet struck me in any visceral way that being nineteen was not a long-term proposition), not only older and wiser but more experienced, more independent, more interesting, more possessed of an exotic past: marriages and the breaking up of marriages, money and the lack of it, sex and politics and the Adriatic seen at dawn; the stuff not only of grown-up life itself but, more poignantly to me at the time, the very stuff which might be transubstantiated into five short stories. I recall a Trotskyist, then in his forties. I recall a young woman who lived, with a barefoot man and a large white dog, in an attic lit only by candles. I recall classroom discussions which ranged over meetings with Paul and Jane Bowles, incidents involving Djuna Barnes, years spent in Paris, in Beverly Hills, in the Yucatán, on the Lower East Side of New York and on Repulse Bay and even on morphine. I had spent seventeen of my nineteen years in Sacramento, and the other two in the Tri Delt house on Warring Street in Berkeley. I had never read Paul or Jane Bowles, let alone met them, and when, some fifteen years later at a friend's house in Santa Monica Canyon, I did meet Paul Bowles, I was immediately rendered as dumb and awestruck as I had been when I was nineteen and taking English 106A.

In short I had no past, and, every Monday-

Wednesday-Friday at noon in Dwinelle Hall, it
seemed increasingly clear to me that I had no
future. I ransacked my closet for clothes in which
I might appear invisible in class, and came up
with only a dirty raincoat. I sat in this raincoat
and I listened to other people's stories read aloud
and I despaired of ever knowing what they knew.
I attended every meeting of this class and never
spoke once. I managed to write only three of the
required five stories. I received—only, I think
now, because Mr. Schorer, a man of infinite kind-
ness to and acuity about his students, divined
intuitively that my failing performance was a
function of adolescent paralysis, of a yearning to
be good and a fright that I never would be, of ter-
ror that any sentence I committed to paper would
expose me as *not good enough*—a course grade
of B. I wrote no more stories for exactly ten years.

When I say I wrote no more stories for exactly
ten years I do not mean that I wrote nothing at
all. In fact I wrote constantly. I wrote, once I left
Berkeley, for a living. I went to New York and
I wrote merchandising copy for *Vogue* and I
wrote promotion copy for *Vogue* (the distinction

between the two was definite but recondite, and to try to explain it would be like giving the AFL-CIO definition of two apparently similar jobs on the line at the Ford assembly plant in Pico Rivera, California) and after a while I wrote editorial copy for *Vogue*. A sample of the last: "Opposite, above: All through the house, colour, verve, improvised treasures in happy but anomalous coexistence. Here, a Frank Stella, an art nouveau stained-glass panel, a Roy Lichtenstein. Not shown: a table covered with frankly brilliant oilcloth, a Mexican find at fifteen cents a yard."

It is easy to make light of this kind of "writing," and I mention it specifically because I do not make light of it at all: it was at *Vogue* that I learned a kind of ease with words, a way of regarding words not as mirrors of my own inadequacy but as tools, toys, weapons to be deployed strategically on a page. In a caption of, say, eight lines, each line to run no more or less than twenty-seven characters, not only every word but every letter counted. At *Vogue* one learned fast, or one did not stay, how to play games with words, how to put a couple of unwieldy dependent clauses through the typewriter and roll them out transformed into one simple sentence composed of precisely thirty-nine characters. We were connoisseurs of synonyms. We were collectors of verbs. (I recall "to ravish" as a highly favored verb for a number of issues and I also recall it, for a number of issues more, as the source of a highly favored noun: "ravishments," as in "tables cluttered with porcelain tulips, Fabergé eggs, other ravishments.") We learned as reflex the grammatical tricks we had learned only as marginal corrections in school ("there were two oranges and an apple" read better than "there were an apple and two oranges," passive verbs slowed down sentences, "it" needed a reference within the scan of the eye), learned to rely on the *OED*, learned to write and rewrite and rewrite again. "Run it through again, sweetie, it's not quite there." "Give me a shock verb two lines in." "Prune it out, clean it up, make the point." Less was more, smooth was better, and absolute precision essential to the monthly grand illusion. Going to work for *Vogue* was, in the late 1950s, not unlike training with the Rockettes.

All of this was tonic, particularly to someone

who had labored for some years under the delusion that to set two sentences side by side was to risk having the result compared widely and unfavorably to *The Golden Bowl*. Gradually I began, in the evenings and between deadlines and in lieu of lunch, to play with words not for *Vogue* but for myself. I began to make notes. I began to write down everything I saw and heard and remembered and imagined. I began to write, or so I thought, another story. I had in mind a story about a woman and a man in New York:

She could no longer concentrate on what he was saying, for she had thought of something that happened in California, the winter she was fifteen. There was no reason why she should remember it this afternoon, yet the recollection carried all that urgent, shining clarity peculiar to things that happened a long time ago in another part of the country. There had been a week of heavy rain that December, and the valley rivers were nearing flood stage. She had been on Christmas vacation, and every morning she would

get up to find the house colder and damper
than it had been the day before. She and her
mother would have breakfast together, looking out the kitchen window into the rain and
watching the water swirl through the gully
which separated their property from Dr.
Wood's. "All the fruit's going," her mother
would say dispassionately every morning at
breakfast. "All the fruit, shot right to hell."
Then she would pour another cup of coffee
and remark resignedly that it was obvious to
her, even if it was not to the army engineers,
that the levees could not hold much longer. Every fifteen minutes the two of them
listened to ominous bulletins on the radio,
telling when and where the rivers were
expected to crest. One morning the Sacramento crested at thirty-one feet, and when
they announced that it would crest the next
day at thirty-eight, the engineers began to
evacuate the ranches upstream. Sometime
during that next morning a levee gave way
forty miles upstream from Sacramento, and
the papers on Christmas Eve showed aerial

photographs of the levee crumbling under sheets of muddy water, and of families huddled in their bathrobes on the tops of houses. The evacuees were streaming into town all that night, to sleep in school gymnasiums and the parish halls of churches.

"What are you going to do," he asked, quite as interested as if he were watching an intensely absorbing play.

"Go to California and work in the fruit," she said dully.

Raining: wet leaves, black streets.

Driving past the Horst ranch, hop strings limp in the rain.

Fulton strip wet and cheap. Fire in Mrs. Miles's: buying a dress to wear to parties.

Watching the rain from windows all over.

On dining room table, silver and linen lying after parties.

Dances.

Bars in the rain where the fire never works.

Any place I hang my hat is home sweet home to me.

.   .   .

So went the "beginning" of this story I had in
mind, this story I believed to be about a woman
and a man in New York—I use the word "beginning" only as shorthand, since nothing so
rough and inchoate can be said to have a true
beginning—and so went some of the notes I
made in an attempt to get down on paper some
of the things I wanted in the story. The notes, tell-
ingly, have nothing to do with a woman and a man
in New York. The notes—that silver lying on the
dining room table after parties, those bars in the
rain where the fire never worked, those figures
about when and where the Sacramento River
would rest—say simply this: *remember*. The notes
reveal that what I actually had on my mind that
year in New York—had *on my mind* as opposed
to *in mind*—was a longing for California, a home-
sickness, a nostalgia so obsessive that nothing else
figured. In order to discover what was on my mind
I needed room. I needed room for the rivers and
for the rain and for the way the almonds came into
blossom around Sacramento, room for irrigation

ditches and room for the fear of kiln fires, room in which to play with everything I remembered and did not understand. In the end I wrote not a story about a woman and a man in New York but a novel about the wife of a hop grower on the Sacramento River. The novel was my first and it was called *Run River* and I did not have it clearly in mind until five years later, when I was finishing it. I suspect that writers of short stories know their own minds rather better than that.

Short stories demand a certain awareness of one's own intentions, a certain narrowing of the focus. Let me give you an example. One morning in 1975 I found myself aboard the 8:45 a.m. Pan American from Los Angeles to Honolulu. There were, before take-off from Los Angeles, "mechanical difficulties," and a half-hour delay. During this delay the stewardesses served coffee and orange juice and two children played tag in the aisles and, somewhere behind me, a man began screaming at a woman who seemed to be his wife. I say that the woman seemed to be his wife only because the tone of his invective sounded practiced, although the only words I heard clearly

were these: "You are driving me to murder." After
a moment I was aware of the door to the plane
being opened a few rows behind me, and of the
man rushing off. There were many Pan American
employees rushing on and off then, and considerable confusion. I do not know whether the man
reboarded the plane before take-off or whether
the woman went on to Honolulu alone, but I
thought about it all the way across the Pacific.
I thought about it while I was drinking a sherry
on the rocks and I thought about it during lunch
and I was still thinking about it when the first of
the Hawaiian Islands appeared off the left wing-
tip. It was not until we had passed Diamond Head
and were coming in low over the reef for landing
at Honolulu, however, that I realized what I most
disliked about this incident: I disliked it because
it had the aspect of a short story, one of those "little epiphany" or "window on the world" stories,
one of those stories in which the main character
glimpses a crisis in a stranger's life—a woman
weeping in a tea room, quite often, or an acci-
dent seen from the window of a train, "tea rooms"
and "trains" still being fixtures of short stories al-

though not of real life—and is moved to see his or her own life in a new light. Again, my dislike was a case of needing room in which to play with what I did not understand. I was not going to Honolulu because I wanted to see life reduced to a short story. I was going to Honolulu because I wanted to see life expanded to a novel, and I still do. I wanted not a window on the world but the world itself. I wanted everything in the picture. I wanted room for flowers, and reef fish, and people who might or might not have been driving one another to murder but in any case were not impelled, by the demands of narrative convention, to say so out loud on the 8:45 a.m. Pan American from Los Angeles to Honolulu.

By way of explaining what moved me to write three short stories in 1964 and none at all—if we except classroom assignments—in any other year, I can suggest only that my first novel had just been published, and I was suffering a fear common among people who have just written a first novel: the fear of never writing another. (As a matter of fact this fear is also common among people who have just written a second novel, a third novel, and, for all I know, a forty-fourth novel, but at the time I considered it a unique affliction.) I sat in front of my typewriter and believed that another subject would never present itself. I believed that I would be forever dry. I believed that I would "forget how." Accordingly, as a kind of desperate finger exercise, I tried writing stories.

I had, and have, no talent for it, no feel for the particular rhythms of short fiction, no ability to focus the world in the window. The first of these stories, "Coming Home," is cast in an extremely simple and highly conventional form: it is one of those stories in which the lives of the characters are meant to be revealed through a single dialogue, a dialogue apparently overheard by a neutral recorder. This form demands absolute control—consider Hemingway's "Hills Like White Elephants" and you will see the form at its best—and "Coming Home" illustrates no control at all. One whole section of the story resembles nothing so much as a studio synopsis of a novel.

What is that Kentucky coal mine doing in the story? Who saw those Impressionist paintings? Who is telling the story? Why was I trying to write this kind of story if I didn't know enough to stick to the rules, do it right, let the dialogue do all the work? My impatience with "Coming Home" applies equally to "The Welfare Island Ferry," a story which differs in technique from "Coming Home" but is, again, a very familiar kind of story. "The Welfare Island Ferry" is a "shock of recognition" story, a story in which the reader is meant to apprehend, late on and quite suddenly, something of which the characters remain unaware. There is in this story a single withheld revelation: one of the characters is demented. My instinct now—and it is an instinct fatal to the story-telling impulse—would be to say, up front, "This girl has gotten herself mixed up with somebody crazy as a loon," and get on with it.

Actually, I am not at all impatient with the third of these stories, "When Did Music Come This Way? Children Dear, Was It Yesterday?" I do not mean to say that I think it is a successful short story: it works not at all as a story. It is instead a

kind of extended notation for an unwritten novel,
an exercise in the truest sense. It was in "When
Did Music" that I taught myself—or began to
teach myself—how to use the first person. It was
in "When Did Music" that I taught myself—or
began to teach myself—how to make narrative
tension out of nothing more than the juxaposi-
tion of past and present. I should have known
what I learned in this story before I ever wrote my
first novel. Had I never written this story I would
have never written a second novel. As crude and
imperfect as the story is, it seems to me by far the
most interesting of the three.

It was also the most difficult of the three to
place. "Coming Home" appeared in *The Saturday Evening Post*. "The Welfare Island Ferry"
appeared in *Harper's Bazaar*. "When Did Music
Come This Way?" appeared nowhere at all for a
long, long time. It was written, curiously enough,
"on commission" from Rust Hills, who was then
the fiction editor at the *Post*. He had called or
written me—I forget which—to say that the *Post*
was planning a "theme" issue about children, an
issue in which every article and story would have

to do—however peripherally—with children. A number of writers had been asked to submit stories for this issue. Each would receive a "guarantee," or minimum payment. Not all of the stories would be accepted. I wrote the story and submitted it. I was represented at the time by the William Morris Agency, and these letters from the Morris office in New York to me in California suggest the troubled course of the story:

October 9, 1964: "As you probably know, Rust wrote to a great many writers regarding stories for a children's issue, and the guarantee for everyone is a flat $200. On the price for the story itself, they will pay $1750, or a $250 increase over your last price. Please let me know whether this is agreeable and if so we'll confirm the terms on your behalf..."

November 30, 1964: "I'm really disappointed not to have better news for you, but Rust Hills has returned WHEN DID MUSIC COME THIS WAY? CHILDREN DEAR, WAS IT YESTERDAY?... We'll of course

send the guarantee check off to you just as
soon as we receive it. Since you indicated
that you wanted to do some further work
on the story, I am wondering whether you
would like the manuscript returned to you
at this point ..."

December 8, 1964: "... I am looking for-
ward to receiving the revised copies of
THE WELFARE ISLAND and WHEN DID
MUSIC COME THIS WAY ..."

December 11, 1964: "... The revised versions
of both stories have gone out—WELFARE
ISLAND to *Bazaar* and WHEN DID MUSIC
COME THIS WAY to *The New Yorker* ..."

April 13, 1965: "... The manuscript is now at
Esquire and I will let you know as soon as we
hear anything further ..."

June 2, 1965: "I'm really sorry there isn't
any good news yet on WHEN DID MUSIC
COME THIS WAY? CHILDREN DEAR,

WAS IT YESTERDAY? Since I wrote you last it has been declined by *Esquire* and *Harper's Bazaar. Bazaar* commented that they love the way you write, but feel MUSIC is not as good as THE WELFARE ISLAND FERRY . . ."

August 2, 1965: "As you know, we've been submitting WHEN DID MUSIC COME THIS WAY? CHILDREN DEAR, WAS IT YESTERDAY? to the magazines, and the following is a list of places where it's been seen. *Saturday Evening Post:* 'Many of us read it and a great many were excited and insistent in their admiration of it. Others, and they include Bill Emerson who has the final vote, also admired it but felt that it was wrong for the *Post,* not so much because of its subject matter, but also because of the oblique method of narration.' *The New Yorker:* 'as a whole it just isn't effective enough.' *Ladies' Home Journal:* 'too negative for us.' *McCall's:* 'I feel very bad about rejecting this story—not because I think it's really a well worked-out story but because the writing is so awfully good. She has a very special way of involving the reader ... but I'm turning this down, reluctantly, because I don't think it's a successful story in the end.' *Good Housekeeping:* 'marvelously written, very real, and so utterly depressing that I'm going to sit under a cloud of angst and gloom all afternoon ... I'm sorry we are seldom inclined to give our readers this bad a time.' *Redbook:* 'just too brittle.' *Atlantic Monthly:* 'I hope you'll be sending us more of Joan Didion's work, but this didn't make it, so back to you.' *Cosmopolitan:* (sent twice due to change in editorial staff) 'too depressing.' *Esquire:* no comment. *Harper's Bazaar:* 'While THE WELFARE ISLAND FERRY is almost my favorite among the stories we have published ... I feel that WHEN DID MUSIC COME THIS WAY? is not quite as good.' *Vogue:* 'not quite right for us.' *Mademoiselle:* 'unable to use this particular story.' *The Reporter:* 'alas, not right for *The Reporter.*' I'm afraid that at this point we can

think of no other markets to which we can
submit it other than the reviews. I would
like to try the story at some of the reviews,
unless you have some other ideas. Would
you let me know, please."

November 7, 1966: "...I had sent it...to
the *Denver Quarterly* who write that they
would like to use it in their fourth issue,
which is due shortly after the first of the
year. Their rate is a miniscule $5 per page
and since the story would run about 10 pages
for them, they would pay $50. Please let me
know whether or not you'd like us to go
ahead with this on your behalf. For the
record, the story was submitted to the following markets before going to *Denver:
Saturday Evening Post, New Yorker, Ladies'
Home Journal, Cosmopolitan, McCall's,
Good Housekeeping, Redbook, Atlantic
Monthly, Cosmopolitan* (resubmitted), *Esquire, Harper's Bazaar, Vogue, Mademoiselle, Reporter, Harper's, Hudson Review,
Kenyon Review, Virginia Quarterly, Ladies'*

Home Journal (resubmitted), *Paris Review*, *Yale Review* and *Sewanee Review*. All best..."

All best indeed. The story appeared in the winter 1967 issue of *The Denver Quarterly*. By winter 1967 I had begun a second novel, and never wrote another story. I doubt that I ever will.

1978

Some Women

Some years ago I had a job, at *Vogue,* which involved going to photographers' studios and watching women being photographed. These were photographs meant not for the fashion but for the "feature" pages of *Vogue,* portraits of women celebrated for one reason or another, known (usually) because they were starring in a movie or appearing in a play or known (less often) because they had pioneered a vaccine or known (more often than we pretended) just because they were known. "Anything at all you're comfortable in," we were instructed to say if the subject ventured to ask what she should wear for the sitting; "We only want you to be yourself." We accepted without question, in other words, the traditional convention of the portrait, which was that some-

how, somewhere, in the transaction between artist and subject, the "truth" about the latter would
be revealed; that the photographer would pen-
etrate and capture some "essence," some secret
of personality or character not apparent to the
naked eye.

In fact what occurred in these sittings, as in all
portrait sittings, was a transaction of an entirely
opposite kind: success was understood to depend
on the extent to which the subject conspired, tac-
itly, to be not "herself" but whoever and whatever
it was that the photographer wanted to see in the
lens. Of those long mornings and afternoons in
the studio (whether the studio was uptown or
downtown, whether it belonged to Irving Penn
or to Bert Stern or to Duane Michals or to one of
a dozen other photographers then shooting fea-
tures for *Vogue,* it was referred to always as just
"the studio," a generic workspace, a syntactical
reflex left from the years when all *Vogue*'s con-
tract photographers worked in the magazine's
own studio) I recall mainly little tricks, small
improvisations, the efforts required to ensure that
the photographer was seeing what he wanted. I

remember one sitting for which the lens was covered with black chiffon. I remember another during which, after the "anything at all" in which the subject had apparently believed herself comfortable had been seen in the Polaroids and declared not what was wanted, I lent the subject my own dress, and worked the rest of the sitting wrapped in my raincoat. Here, then, was an early lesson: there would be in each such photograph a "subject," the woman in the studio, and there would also be a subject, and the two would not necessarily intersect.

This business of the subject is tricky. Whether they are painters or photographers or composers or choreographers or for that matter writers, people whose work it is to make something out of nothing do not much like to talk about what they do or how they do it. They will talk quite freely about the technical tricks involved in what they do, about lighting and filters if they are photographers, about voice and tone and rhythm if they are writers, but not about content. The attempt to analyze one's work, which is to say to know one's subject, is seen as destructive. Superstition prevails, fear that the fragile unfinished something will shatter, vanish, revert to the nothing from which it was made. Jean Cocteau once described all such work as deriving from "a profound indolence, a somnolence in which we indulge ourselves like invalids who try to prolong dreams." In dreams we do not analyze the action, or it vanishes. Gabriel García Márquez once spoke to *The New York Times* about the "bad luck" that would befall him were he to discuss the novel he was then writing; he meant of course that the novel would go away, lose its power to compel his imagination. I once knew I "had" a novel when it presented itself to me as an oil slick, with an iridescent surface; during the several years it took me to finish the novel I mentioned the oil slick to no one, afraid the talismanic hold the image had on me would fade, go flat, go away, like a dream told at breakfast. "If you say too much you lose some of that mystery," Robert Mapplethorpe once told a BBC interviewer who wanted to talk about his work. "You want to be able to pick up on the magic of the moment. That's the rush of doing photography. You don't know why it's happening but it's happening."

One question: If Robert Mapplethorpe's "subjects" here are women, what then is his subject? One answer: His subject is the same as it was when his "subjects" were the men in leather, or the flowers, or the Coral Sea on a low horizon. *You don't know why it's happening but it's happening.* "I was a Catholic boy," he also told the BBC. "I went to church every Sunday. The way I arrange things is very Catholic. It's always been that way when I put things together. Very symmetrical."

Of the women Robert Mapplethorpe chose to photograph during the course of his career, most were well known, figures of considerable celebrity or fashion or achievement. There were models and there were actresses. There were singers, dancers, choreographers; makers of art and dealers in art. Most were New York women, with the familiar New York edge. Most were conventionally "pretty," even "beautiful," or rendered so not only by the artifices of light and makeup but by the way they presented themselves to the camera: They were professional women, performers before the camera. They were women who knew how to make their way in the world. They were women

who knew a lot of things, and what they knew did
not, on the evidence, encourage certainty. Some
met the camera with closed eyes, as in a carnal
swoon, or Victorian faint. Others confronted it
so directly as to seem startled into a fleeting mad-
ness; these would seem to have been inhabitants
of a world in which survival depended on the ability to seduce, beguile, conspire, deceive. *Sing for
your supper,* something in these photographs tells
us, *and you'll get breakfast.*

Songbirds always eat: this is not a "modern"
idea, nor did the women in Mapplethorpe photographs present themselves to us as modern
women. There were in some of his photographs
the familiar nineteenth-century images of domi-
nation and submission, the erotic discomforts of
straps and leather and five-inch heels, of those
shoes that cause the wearer's flesh to wrinkle at
the instep. There were doomed virgins (downcast
eyes, clasped hands), and intimations of mortality,
skin like marble, faces like masques, a supernatu-
ral radiance, the phosphorescent glow we sometimes attribute to angels, and to decaying flesh.

The idealization here was never of the present.

Mapplethorpe photographs meant to sell bath-
ing suits suggested not the athleticism associated
with an idealized present, not freedom of move-
ment at all, but bondage, and spanking, the sexual
dreams of imperial England. The familiar face of
Grace Jones, as photographed by Mapplethorpe,
suggested not the androgynous future for which
it had come to stand but the nineteenth-century
passion for the exotic, the romance with Africa,
with Egypt. A Mapplethorpe fashion photograph,
the naked black "Thomas" dancing with the spec-
trally white "Dovanna," suggested classical ballet,
the pas de deux in which the betrayer courts the
betrayed, back from the grave, the prima ballerina
from the dance of the shades.

Even little girls, as photographed by Mapplethorpe, seemed Victorian, not children in
the modern sense but sentient beings, creatures
with barrettes and bunnies but nonetheless grave
with responsibility; small adults, who gazed at
us with the utter clarity of what they knew and did
not yet know. Perversely, of all the women Robert
Mapplethorpe photographed, perhaps only Yoko
Ono presented herself as "modern," entirely in

charge of herself, a woman who had negotiated the demands of sex and celebrity to appear before us as a middle-aged survivor, with sensible lapels, clear eyes, blown hair. There was something interesting in all of this, and willful, and the will was not that of the "subjects."

There was always about Robert Mapplethorpe an astonishing convergence of quite romantic impulses. There was the romance of the apparently unconventional. There was the romance of art for its own sake. There was the willingness to test the outer reaches of the possible, to explore the "interesting" ("I just thought it would be an interesting idea, having a ring through your tit," he told the BBC about the early film *Robert Having His Nipple Pierced,* the romance of the edge). There was the romance of the Catholic boy from the lower-middle-class reaches of Queens ("It wasn't what I wanted," he once said about that) who came to the city and broke on through to the other side, reinvented himself as a Rimbaud of the baths.

That romantic agony should have been revived as the downtown style in the greatest bourgeois city in the modern world at the moment of its decline was, in any historical sense, predictable, and yet Robert Mapplethorpe's work has often been seen as an aesthetic sport, so entirely outside any historical or social context, and so "new," as to resist interpretation. This "newness" has in fact become so fixed an idea about Mapplethorpe that we tend to overlook the source of his strength, which derived, from the beginning, less from the shock of the new than from the shock of the old, from the rather unnerving novelty of exposure to a fixed moral universe. There was always in his work the tension, even the struggle, between light and dark. There was the exaltation of powerlessness. There was the seductiveness of death, the fantasy of crucifixion.

There was, above all, the perilous imposition of order on chaos, of classical form on unthinkable images. *It's always been that way when I put things together. Very symmetrical.* "I don't like that particular word, 'shocking.'" Robert Mapplethorpe told *ARTnews* in late 1988, when he was struggling with illness and was asked one more time to discuss the famous leather photographs.

"I'm looking for the unexpected. I'm looking for things I've never seen before. But I have trouble with the word 'shocking' because I'm not really shocked by anything—I was in a position to take those pictures. I felt an obligation to do them." This is the voice of someone whose subject was finally that very symmetry with which he himself had arranged things.

1989

The Long-Distance Runner

There are in my husband's and my house two photographs of Tony Richardson. In the earlier of the two, taken in what must have been 1981, he is riding a dolly on which is mounted a Panaflex camera, somewhere near El Paso, a man deliriously engaged by—besotted by, transformed by—the act of making a picture, in this instance a "big" picture, the kind of picture on which every day the camera rolls costs tens of thousands of dollars, the kind of picture on which the dailies get flown to the studio every night and everyone in the projection room tenses a little when the take numbers flash on the screen, a picture with a big crew and a bankable star, Jack Nicholson, *The Border*. The more recent photograph was taken on an exterior location in Spain during the late fall of 1989. What

appears to be a master shot is in progress. We see
the camera operator, the sound boom, the reflec-
tor. We see the actors, James Woods and Melanie
Griffith. And, over in the far left of the frame, in
jeans and tennis shoes and a red parka, we see the
director, a man visibly less well than he seemed
riding the dolly outside El Paso but just as deliriously engaged by—besotted by, transformed
by—the act of making a picture, in this case a
twenty-one-minute film for television, an adap-
tation of Ernest Hemingway's "Hills Like White
Elephants" for HBO.

I never knew anyone who so loved to make
things, or anyone who had such limited interest
in what he had already made. What Tony loved
was the sheer act of doing it: whether what he was
making was a big picture or theater or twenty-
one minutes for television, its particular nature
or potential success or potential audience was
to him irrelevant, of no interest, not in the least
the point. The purity of his enthusiasm for making, say, an *As You Like It* to run for a few nights
at a community theater in Long Beach, or an
Antony and Cleopatra starring television actors

at a theater in downtown Los Angeles, was total: the notion that these projects might have less intrinsic potential than the productions of the same plays he had done in London with Vanessa Redgrave remained alien to him. "Something absolutely magical happens at the end," I remember him promising about the downtown *Antony and Cleopatra*. He was talking not about his work but about *working,* about everyone making the moment together in some larger proscenium. "Everything is magic, a dream," I remember him announcing when he called from Spain to ask for a minor adjustment (the script, which my husband and I had written, called for the principals to wade in a stream, but the available stream was too cold) on "Hills Like White Elephants." He was talking, again, not about his work but about working, about that suspended state of being in which the cold stream and the olive grove and the not entirely well man in the red parka could be composed and recomposed, controlled, remembered just that way.

"Magic" was what Tony always wanted, in life as in work, and, like most people who love what they do, he made no distinctions between the two. "I want it to be magic," he would say, whether he was planning a picture or an improvised theatrical at his house or a moonlight picnic on the beach: he wanted magic, and he made it, and in the interests of making it he would mortgage his house, put up his own completion bonds, start shooting on the eve of an actors' strike. When he was not making a picture or theater he would make the same kind of magic happen at home: a lunch or a dinner or a summer was for him raw footage, something to shoot and see how it printed. His house was a set, filled with flowers and birds and sunlight and children, with old loves and current loves, with every conceivable confrontational possibility; forests of Arden, Prospero's island, a director's conceit. "Come to France with me in July," I recall him saying one night at dinner, and when my husband and I said we could not, he turned to our daughter, then fourteen, and announced that in that case she would come alone. She did. There seemed to be dozens of people in Tony's conceit that July, and by the time we arrived to pick up Quintana she was swimming topless in St. Tropez, dancing all night, speaking French, and was being courted by two Italians under the misapprehension that she was on vacation from UCLA. "This has been absolutely magical," Tony said.

It was also in the interests of making this magic that Tony could be so famously dogmatic, contrary, relentlessly ready to strand himself on whatever limb seemed likely to draw lightning. Quite often, for example, I heard him speak emphatically and enthusiastically about the virtues of "colorizing" black-and-white motion pictures, in each case to someone who had just signed a letter or written an op-ed piece or obtained an injunction opposing colorization. "If they had had color, they would have shot color," he would say, emphasizing each syllable equally, the declarative enunciation that gave him what John Osborne once described as "the most imitated voice in his profession." *That is just pretentious nonsense. Color is better.* On two occasions I heard him rise to a passionate defense of the tennis player John McEnroe, who had done, Tony declared, "the most glorious thing" by throwing down his racket in a match at Wimbledon; the case Tony made derived partly, of course, from his quite fundamental anarchism, his essential loathing of the English class system and attendant sporting rituals.

Yet it derived equally from a simple wish to provoke the listener, structure the evening, make the scene work. Tony thrived on the very moments most of us try to avoid. Social consensus was to him unthinkable, stifling, everything he had left behind. Raised voices were the stuff of theater, of freedom. I remember him calling on the morning after a dinner in Beverly Hills that had abruptly become a shambles when my husband and an old friend, Brian Moore, began shouting at each other. There had been eight at the table (six, after my husband walked out and I fled), including Tony, whose delight in the turn the dinner had taken seemed absolute: the fight was the unexpected "magic" of the evening, the quiet dinner among friends dissolving into peril, the dramatic possibility realized.

I thought of the first sheep I ever remember seeing—hundreds of them, and how our car drove suddenly into them on the back lot of the old Laemmle studio. They were unhappy about being in pictures, but the men in the car with us kept saying:

"Is that what you wanted, Dick?"

"Isn't that swell?" And the man named Dick kept standing up in the car as if he were Cortez or Balboa, looking over that gray fleecy undulation.

—F. SCOTT FITZGERALD, *The Last Tycoon*

Tony died, of a neurological infection resulting from AIDS, at St. Vincent's Hospital in Los Angeles on the fourteenth of November, 1991. He had begun this book some years before, during one of the many periods when he was waiting for one or another script or element or piece of financing to fall into place so that he could once again stand up in the car as if he were Cortez or Balboa and look out over whatever it was he wanted to make. Most people who make pictures learn to endure these periods of enforced idleness, some better than others, and since Tony was one of the others, he tended during such periods to multiply whatever balls he had in the air, commission a new script,

meet one last time with the moneyman, undertake
some particularly arduous excursion ("You just
don't like to have fun," he said accusingly when I
declined to consider a weekend trip that involved
cholera shots), *improve the moment.* Writing this
book, he said on the evening he first mentioned it,
was "something to do," and then he did not mention it again. When we asked, some time later, he
said that he had abandoned it. "It is worthless," I
remember him saying. "Absolutely worthless."
Whether he believed that the book was worthless,
or that the act of writing it was worthless, or that
looking back itself was worthless, I never knew.

Nor did I know, until the afternoon of the day
he died, when someone who had typed for him
gave his daughters this manuscript, that he had
finished the book, and I am still not at all sure
when he finished it. The book does not deal with
the work he did during the seven years between
The Hotel New Hampshire and the time he died,
and he mentions in the closing pages that he is
fifty-seven, which would seem to suggest that he
wrote them six years before he died, yet there is
about those closing pages a finality, an uncharac-
teristic sense of *adieu.* This was not a man who

had much interest in looking back. Nor was this a man afflicted by despair; the only time I ever saw him wretched was when he perceived a sadness or pain or even a moment of fleeting uncertainty in one of his daughters. And yet he wrote:

> Snapshots of my three daughters look directly at me from a bulletin board as I'm writing. And as one of their gazes makes contact they seem to be asking the one question—what's ahead? In the theatre just as there's a well-known superstition you can't ever quote or mention "the Scottish play" *Macbeth* without bringing bad luck, there's also a superstition that you should never say the last word or the last couplet of a Restoration play until the first night. I'm finding this as hard to finish as to say that last word. I can say to Natasha and Joely and Katharine I love them very much, but I sense they want more.

Did he know for six years that he was dying? Or would he say that to speak of "dying" in that sense is sentimental nonsense, since we are all dying?

"There isn't an answer," he wrote earlier in this book about learning something he had not known about someone he loved. "Just a kind of spooky sadness—angels passing over us, or like that moment in Act II of *The Cherry Orchard* when Madame Ranevsky hears a distant sound like the string of a violin snapping." I suppose there were not many weeks during those six years when we did not talk or have lunch or spend an evening together. We spent holidays together. His daughter Natasha was married in our house. I loved him. And yet I have no idea.

1993

Last Words

*In the late summer of that year we lived in a house
in a village that looked across the river and the
plain to the mountains. In the bed of the river there
were pebbles and boulders, dry and white in the sun,
and the water was clear and swiftly moving and
blue in the channels. Troops went by the house and
down the road and the dust they raised powdered
the leaves of the trees. The trunks of the trees too
were dusty and the leaves fell early that year and
we saw the troops marching along the road and the
dust rising and leaves, stirred by the breeze, falling
and the soldiers marching and afterward the road
bare and white except for the leaves.*

So goes the famous first paragraph of Ernest
Hemingway's *A Farewell to Arms,* which I was
moved to reread by the recent announcement
that what was said to be Hemingway's last novel
would be published posthumously next year. That
paragraph, which was published in 1929, bears
examination: four deceptively simple sentences,

126 words, the arrangement of which remains as mysterious and thrilling to me now as it did when I first read them, at twelve or thirteen, and imagined that if I studied them closely enough and practiced hard enough I might one day arrange 126 such words myself. Only one of the words has three syllables. Twenty-two have two. The other 103 have one. Twenty-four of the words are "the," fifteen are "and." There are four commas. The liturgical cadence of the paragraph derives in part from the placement of the commas (their presence in the second and fourth sentences, their absence in the first and third), but also from that repetition of "the" and of "and," creating a rhythm so pronounced that the omission of "the" before the word "leaves" in the fourth sentence ("and we saw the troops marching along the road and the dust rising and leaves, stirred by the breeze, falling") casts exactly what it was meant to cast, a chill, a premonition, a foreshadowing of the story to come, the awareness that the author has already shifted his attention from late summer to a darker season. The power of the paragraph, offering as it does the illusion but not the fact of specific-

ity, derives precisely from this kind of deliberate omission, from the tension of withheld information. In the later summer of *what* year? *What* river, *what* mountains, *what* troops?

We all know the "life" of the man who wrote that paragraph. The rather reckless attractions of the domestic details became fixed in the national memory stream: *Ernest and Hadley have no money, so they ski at Cortina all winter. Pauline comes to stay. Ernest and Hadley are at odds with each other over Pauline, so they all take refuge at Juan-les-Pins. Pauline catches cold, and recuperates at the Waldorf-Astoria.* We have seen the snapshots: the celebrated author fencing with the bulls at Pamplona, fishing for marlin off Havana, boxing at Bimini, crossing the Ebro with the Spanish loyalists, kneeling beside "his" lion or "his" buffalo or "his" oryx on the Serengeti Plain. We have observed the celebrated author's survivors, read his letters, deplored or found lessons in his excesses, in his striking of attitudes, in the humiliations of his claim to personal machismo, in the degradations both derived from and revealed by his apparent tolerance for his own celebrity.

"This is to tell you about a young man named Ernest Hemingway, who lives in Paris (an American), writes for the *transatlantic review* and has a brilliant future," F. Scott Fitzgerald wrote to Maxwell Perkins in 1924. "I'd look him up right away. He's the real thing." By the time "the real thing" had seen his brilliant future both realized and ruined, he had entered the valley of extreme emotional fragility, of depressions so grave that by February of 1961, after the first of what would be two courses of shock treatment, he found himself unable to complete even the single sentence he had agreed to contribute to a ceremonial volume for President John F. Kennedy. Early on the Sunday morning of July 2, 1961, the celebrated author got out of his bed in Ketchum, Idaho, went downstairs, took a double-barrelled Boss shotgun from a storage room in the cellar, and emptied both barrels into the center of his forehead. "I went downstairs," his fourth wife, Mary Welsh Hemingway, reported in her 1976 memoir, *How It Was,* "saw a crumpled heap of bathrobe and blood, the shotgun lying in the disintegrated flesh, in the front vestibule of the sitting room."

.   .   .

The didactic momentum of the biography was such that we sometimes forgot that this was a writer who had in his time made the English language new, changed the rhythms of the way both his own and the next few generations would speak and write and think. The very grammar of a Hemingway sentence dictated, or was dictated by, a certain way of looking at the world, a way of looking but not joining, a way of moving through but not attaching, a kind of romantic individual-ism distinctly adapted to its time and source. If we bought into those sentences, we would see the troops marching along the road, but we would not necessarily march with them. We would report, but not join. We would make, as Nick Adams made in the Nick Adams stories and as Frederic Henry made in *A Farewell to Arms,* a separate peace: "In the fall the war was always there, but we did not go to it any more."

So pervasive was the effect of this Hemingway diction that it became the voice not only of his admirers but even of those whose approach to the

world was in no way grounded in romantic indi-
vidualism. I recall being surprised, when I was
teaching George Orwell in a class at Berkeley in
1975, by how much of Hemingway could be heard
in his sentences. "The hills opposite us were grey
and wrinkled like the skins of elephants," Orwell
had written in *Homage to Catalonia* in 1938. "The
hills across the valley of the Ebro were long and
white," Hemingway had written in "Hills Like
White Elephants" in 1927. "A mass of Latin words
falls upon the facts like soft snow, blurring the outlines and covering up all the details," Orwell had
written in "Politics and the English Language"
in 1946. "I was always embarrassed by the words
sacred, glorious, and sacrifice and the expression
in vain," Hemingway had written in *A Farewell to
Arms* in 1929. "There were many words that you
could not stand to hear and finally only the names
of places had dignity."

This was a man to whom words mattered.
He worked at them, he understood them, he got
inside them. When he was twenty-four years old
and reading submissions to Ford Madox Ford's
Transatlantic Review he would sometimes try

rewriting them, just for practice. His wish to be survived by only the words he determined fit for publication would have seemed clear enough. "I remember Ford telling me that a man should always write a letter thinking of how it would read to posterity," he wrote to Arthur Mizener in 1950. "This made such a bad impression on me that I burned every letter in the flat including Ford's." In a letter dated May 20, 1958, addressed "To my Executors" and placed in his library safe at La Finca Vigía, he wrote, "It is my wish that none of the letters written by me during my lifetime shall be published. Accordingly, I hereby request and direct you not to publish or consent to the publication by others of any such letters."

His widow and executor, Mary Welsh Hemingway, describing the burden of this restriction as one that "caused me continuous trouble, and disappointment to others," eventually chose to violate it, publishing excerpts from certain letters in *How It Was* and granting permission to Carlos Baker to publish some six hundred others in his *Ernest Hemingway: Selected Letters, 1917–1961.* "There can be no question about the wisdom and

rightness of the decision," Baker wrote, for the
letters "will not only instruct and entertain the
general reader but also provide serious students
of literature with the documents necessary to the
continuing investigation of the life and achieve-
ments of one of the giants of twentieth-century
American fiction."

The peculiarity of being a writer is that the
entire enterprise involves the mortal humiliation
of seeing one's own words in print. The risk of
publication is the grave fact of the life, and, even
among writers less inclined than Hemingway
to construe words as the manifest expression of
personal honor, the notion that words one has not
risked publishing should be open to "continuing
investigation" by "serious students of literature"
could not be calculated to kindle enthusiasm.
"Nobody likes to be tailed," Hemingway himself had in 1952 advised one such investigator,
Charles A. Fenton of Yale, who on the evidence of
the letters was tormenting Hemingway by sending him successive drafts of what would be *The
Apprenticeship of Ernest Hemingway: The Early
Years.* "You do not like to be tailed, investigated,

queried about, by any amateur detective no matter how scholarly or how straight. You ought to be
able to see that, Fenton." A month later Hemingway tried again. "I think you ought to drop the
entire project," he wrote to Fenton, adding, "It
is impossible to arrive at any truth without the
co-operation of the person involved. That co-
operation involves very nearly as much effort
as for a man to write his autobiography." A few
months later, he was still trying:

> In the first page or pages of your Mss. I found
> so many errors of fact that I could spend the
> rest of this winter re-writing and giving you
> the true gen and I would not be able to write
> anything of my own at all. . . . Another thing:
> You have located unsigned pieces by me
> through pay vouchers. But you do not know
> which pieces were changed or re-written by
> the copy desk and which were not. I know
> nothing worse for a writer than for his early
> writing which has been re-written and
> altered to be published without permission
> as his own.

Actually I know few things worse than for another writer to collect a fellow writer's journalism which his fellow writer has elected not to preserve because it is worthless and publish it.

Mr. Fenton I feel very strongly about this. I have written you so before and I write you now again. Writing that I do not wish to publish, you have no right to publish. I would no more do a thing like that to you than I would cheat a man at cards or rifle his desk or wastebasket or read his personal letters.

It might seem safe to assume that a writer who commits suicide has been less than entirely engaged by the work he leaves unfinished, yet there appears to have been not much question about what would happen to the unfinished Hemingway manuscripts. These included not only "the Paris stuff" (as he called it), or *A Moveable Feast* (as Scribner's called it), which Hemingway had in fact shown to Scribner's in 1959 and then withdrawn for revision, but also the novels later published under the titles *Islands in the Stream* and *The Garden of Eden,* several Nick Adams stories, what Mrs. Hemingway called the "original treatment" of the bullfighting pieces published by *Life* before Hemingway's death (this became *The Dangerous Summer*), and what she described as "his semi-fictional account of our African safari," three selections from which she had published in *Sports Illustrated* in 1971 and 1972.

What followed was the systematic creation of a marketable product, a discrete body of work different in kind from, and in fact tending to obscure, the body of work published by Hemingway in his lifetime. So successful was the process of branding this product that in October, according to the House & Home section of *The New York Times,* Thomasville Furniture Industries introduced an "Ernest Hemingway Collection" at the International Home Furnishings Market in High Point, North Carolina, offering "96 pieces of living, dining and bedroom furniture and accessories" in four themes, "Kenya," "Key West," "Havana," and "Ketchum." "We don't have many heroes today," Marla A. Metzner, the president of Fashion Licensing of America, told the *Times.* "We're going back to the great icons of the century, as heroic brands." Ms. Metzner, according to the *Times,* not only "cre-

ated the Ernest Hemingway brand with Hemingway's three sons, Jack, Gregory and Patrick," but
"also represents F. Scott Fitzgerald's grandchil-
dren, who have asked for a Fitzgerald brand."

That this would be the logical outcome of
posthumous marketing cannot have been entirely clear to Mary Welsh Hemingway. During
Hemingway's lifetime, she appears to have remained cool to the marketing impulses of A. E.
Hotchner, whose thirteen-year correspondence
with Hemingway gives the sense that he regarded
the failing author not as the overextended and
desperate figure the letters suggest but as an infinite resource, a mine to be worked, an element
to be packaged into his various entertainment
and publishing "projects." The widow tried to
stop the publication of Hotchner's *Papa Hemingway,* and, although the correspondence makes
clear that Hemingway himself had both trusted
and relied heavily on its author, presented him
in her own memoir mainly as a kind of personal
assistant, a fetcher of manuscripts, an arranger of
apartments, a Zelig apparition in crowd scenes:
"When the *Ile de France* docked in the Hudson
River at noon, March 27, we were elated to find

Charlie Sweeny, my favorite general, awaiting us, together with Lillian Ross, Al Horowitz, Hotchner and some others."

In this memoir, which is memorable mainly for the revelation of its author's rather trying mixture of quite striking competence and strategic incompetence (she arrives in Paris on the day it is liberated and scores a room at the Ritz, but seems bewildered by the domestic problem of how to improve the lighting of the dining room at La Finca Vigía), Mary Welsh Hemingway shared her conviction, at which she appears to have arrived in the face of considerable contrary evidence, that her husband had "clearly" expected her to publish "some, if not all, of his work." The guidelines she set for herself in this task were instructive: "Except for punctuation and the obviously overlooked 'ands' and 'buts' we would present his prose and poetry to readers as he wrote it, letting the gaps lie where they were."

Well, there you are. You care about the punctuation or you don't, and Hemingway did. You care about the "ands" and the "buts" or you don't, and Hemingway did. You think something is in shape to be published or you don't, and Hemingway didn't. "This is it; there are no more books," Charles Scribner III told *The New York Times* by way of announcing the "Hemingway novel" to be published in July of 1999, to celebrate the centennial year of his birth. This piece of work, for which the title *True at First Light* was chosen from the text ("In Africa a thing is true at first light and a lie by noon and you have no more respect for it than for the lovely, perfect weed-fringed lake you see across the sun-baked salt plain"), is said to be the novel on which Hemingway was trying intermittently to work between 1954, when he and Mary Welsh Hemingway returned from the safari in Kenya which provides its narrative, and his suicide in 1961.

This "African novel" seems to have presented at first only the resistance that characterizes the early stage of any novel. In September of 1954, Hemingway wrote to Bernard Berenson from Cuba about the adverse effect of air conditioning on this thing he was doing: "You get the writing done but it's as false as though it were done in the reverse of a greenhouse. Probably I will throw it all away, but maybe when the mornings are alive again I can use the skeleton of what I have written and fill it in with the smells and the early noises of the birds and all the lovely things of this finca which are in the cold months very much like Africa." In September of 1955, he wrote again to Berenson, this time on a new typewriter, explaining that he could not use his old one "because it has page 594 of the [African] book in it, covered over with the dust cover, and it is unlucky to take the pages out." In November of 1955, he reported to Harvey Breit, of *The New York Times,* "Am on page 689 and wish me luck kid." In January of 1956, he wrote to his attorney, Alfred Rice, that he had reached page 810.

There then falls, in the *Selected Letters,* a certain silence on the matter of this African novel. Eight hundred and ten pages or no, there comes a point at which every writer knows when a book is not working, and every writer also knows when the reserves of will and energy and memory and concentration required to make the thing work simply may not be available. "You just have to *go*

on when it is worst and most helpless—there is
only one thing to do with a novel and that is go
straight on through to the end of the damn thing,"
Hemingway had written to F. Scott Fitzgerald in
1929, when Fitzgerald was blocked on the novel
that would be published in 1934 as *Tender Is the
Night.*

In 1929, Hemingway was thirty. His concentration, or his ability to "*go on* when it is worst
and most helpless," was still such that he had
continued rewriting *A Farewell to Arms* while
trying to deal, in the aftermath of his father's
suicide in December of 1928, with the concerns
of his mother, his sixteen-year-old sister, and his
thirteen-year-old brother. "Realize of course that
thing for me to do is not worry but get to work—
finish my book properly so I can help them out
with the proceeds," he had written to Maxwell
Perkins within days of his father's funeral, and six
weeks later he delivered the finished manuscript.
He had seen one marriage destroyed, but not
yet three. He was not yet living with the residue
of the two 1954 plane crashes that had ruptured
his liver, his spleen, and one of his kidneys, col-

lapsed his lower intestine, crushed a vertebra, left first-degree burns on his face and head, and caused concussion and losses of vision and hearing. "Alfred this was a very rough year even before we smashed up in the air-craft," he wrote to Alfred Rice, who had apparently questioned his tax deductions for the African safari:

> But I have a diamond mine if people will let me alone and let me dig the stones out of the blue mud and then cut and polish them. If I can do it I will make more money for the Government than any Texas oilman that gets his depreciation. But I have been beat-up worse than you can be and still be around and I should be working steadily on getting better and then write and not think nor worry about anything else.

"The literal details of writing," Norman Mailer once told an interviewer, "involve one's own physiology or metabolism. You begin from a standing start and have to accelerate yourself to the point of cerebration where the words are coming—well, and in order. All writing is generated by a certain minimum of ego: you must assume a position of authority in saying that the way I'm writing it is the only way it happened. Writer's block, for example, is simply a failure of ego." In August of 1956, Hemingway advised Charles Scribner, Jr., that he had "found it impossible to resume work on the Africa book without some disciplinary writing," and so was writing short stories.

In November of 1958, he mentioned to one of his children that he wanted to "finish book" during a winter stay in Ketchum, but the "book" at issue was now "the Paris stuff." In April of 1960, he told Scribner to scratch this still untitled Paris book from the fall list: "Plenty of people will probably think that we have no book and that it is like all the outlines that Scott had and borrowed money on that he never could have finished but you know that if I did not want the chance to make it even better it could be published exactly as you saw it with a few corrections of Mary's typing." Ten months later, and five months before his death, in a letter written to his editor at Scribner's between the two courses of shock treatment administered to him at the Mayo Clinic in Rochester, Minnesota, the writer tried, alarmingly, to explain what he was doing:

> Have material arranged as chapters—they come to 18—and am working on the last one—No *19*—also working on title. This is very difficult. (Have my usual long list—something wrong with all of them but am working toward it—Paris has been used so often it blights anything.) In pages typed they run 7, 14, 5, 6, 9½, 6, 11, 9, 8, 9, 4½, 3½, 8, 10½, 14½, 38½, 10, 3, 3: 177 pages + 5½ pages + 1¼ pages.

I recall listening, some years ago at a dinner party in Berkeley, to a professor of English present *The Last Tycoon* as irrefutable proof that F. Scott Fitzgerald was a bad writer. The assurance with which this judgment was offered so stunned me that I had let it slip into the *donnée* of the evening before I managed to object. *The Last Tycoon*, I said, was an unfinished book, one we had no way

of judging because we had no way of knowing
how Fitzgerald might have finished it. But of
course we did, another guest said, and others
joined in: We had Fitzgerald's "notes," we had
Fitzgerald's "outline," the thing was "entirely laid
out." Only one of us at the table that evening, in
other words, saw a substantive difference between
writing a book and making notes for it, or "outlin-
ing it," or "laying it out."

The most chilling scene ever filmed must be,
for a writer, that moment in *The Shining* when
Shelley Duvall looks at the manuscript on which
her husband has been working and sees, typed
over and over again on each of the hundreds of
pages, only the single line: "All work and no play
makes Jack a dull boy." The manuscript for what
became *True at First Light* was, as Hemingway
left it, some 850 pages long. The manuscript as
edited for publication is half that. This editing
was done by Hemingway's son Patrick, who has
said that he limited his editing to condensing
(which inevitably works to alter what the author
may have intended, as anyone who has been con-
densed knows), changing only some of the place

names, which may or may not have seemed a logical response to the work of the man who wrote, "There were many words that you could not stand to hear and finally only the names of places had dignity."

This question of what should be done with what a writer leaves unfinished goes back to, and is conventionally answered by, citing works we might have lost had the dying wishes of their authors been honored. Virgil's *Aeneid* is mentioned. Franz Kafka's *The Trial* and *The Castle* are mentioned. In 1951, clearly shadowed by mortality, Hemingway judged that certain parts of a long four-part novel on which he had been working for a number of years were sufficiently "finished" to be published after his death, and specified his terms, which did not include the intrusion of any editorial hand and specifically excluded the publication of the unfinished first section. "The last two parts need no cutting at all," he wrote to Charles Scribner in 1951. "The third part needs quite a lot but it is very careful scalpel work and would need no cutting if I were dead. . . . The reason that I wrote you that you could always publish the last three parts sepa-

rately is because I know you can in case through
accidental death or any sort of death I should not
be able to get the first part in proper shape to
publish."

Hemingway himself, the following year, published the fourth part of this manuscript sepa-
rately, as *The Old Man and the Sea.* The "first part"
of the manuscript, the part not yet "in proper
shape to publish," was, after his death, nonetheless published, as part of *Islands in the Stream.*
In the case of the "African novel," or *True at
First Light,* 850 pages reduced by half by someone other than their author can go nowhere the
author intended them to go, but they can provide
the occasion for a chat-show hook, a faux contro-
versy over whether the part of the manuscript in
which the writer on safari takes a Wakamba bride
does or does not reflect a "real" event. The increas-
ing inability of many readers to construe fiction
as anything other than roman à clef, or the raw
material of biography, is both indulged and encouraged. *The New York Times,* in its announcement of the publication of the manuscript, quoted
Patrick Hemingway to this spurious point: " 'Did

Ernest Hemingway have such an experience?'
he said from his home in Bozeman, Montana. 'I
can tell you from all I know—and I don't know
everything—he did not.'"

This is a denial of the idea of fiction, just as the
publication of unfinished work is a denial of the
idea that the role of the writer in his or her work
is to make it. Those excerpts from *True at First
Light* already published can be read only as something not yet made, notes, scenes in the process of
being set down, words set down but not yet written. There are arresting glimpses here and there,
fragments shored against what the writer must
have seen as his ruin, and a sympathetic reader
might well believe it possible that had the writer
lived (which is to say had the writer found the will
and energy and memory and concentration) he
might have shaped the material, written it into
being, made it work as the story the glimpses suggest, that of a man returning to a place he loved
and finding himself at three in the morning con-
fronting the knowledge that he is no longer the
person who loved it and will never now be the
person he had meant to be. But of course such a

possibility would have been in the end closed to this particular writer, for he had already written that story, in 1936, and called it "The Snows of Kilimanjaro." "Now he would never write the things that he had saved to write until he knew enough to write them well," the writer in "The Snows of Kilimanjaro" thought as he lay dying of gangrene in Africa. And then, this afterthought, the saddest story: "Well, he would not have to fail at trying to write them either."

1998

Everywoman.com

According to "The Web Guide to Martha Stewart—The UNOFFICIAL Site!," which was created by a former graduate student named Kerry Ogata as "a thesis procrastination technique" and then passed on to those who now maintain it, the fifty-eight-year-old chairman and CEO of Martha Stewart Living Omnimedia LLC ("MSO" on the New York Stock Exchange) needs only four hours of sleep a night, utilizes the saved hours by grooming her six cats and gardening by flashlight, prefers Macs in the office and a PowerBook for herself, commutes between her house in Westport and her two houses in East Hampton and her Manhattan apartment in a GMC Suburban ("with chauffeur") or a Jaguar XJ6 ("she drives herself"), was raised the second-oldest of six children in a

Polish-American family in Nutley, New Jersey, has one daughter, Alexis, and survived "a non-amicable divorce" from her husband of twenty-six years, Andrew Stewart ("Andy" on the site), who then "married Martha's former assistant who is 21 years younger than he is."

Contributors to the site's "Opinions" page, like good friends everywhere, have mixed feelings about Andy's defection, which occurred in 1987, while Martha was on the road promoting *Martha Stewart Weddings,* the preface to which offered a possibly prescient view of her own 1961 wedding. "I was a naïve nineteen-year-old, still a student at Barnard, and Andy was beginning Yale Law School, so it seemed appropriate to be married in St. Paul's Chapel at Columbia in an Episcopalian service, mainly because we didn't have anyplace else to go," she wrote, and included a photograph showing the wedding dress she and her mother had made of embroidered Swiss organdy bought on West Thirty-eighth Street. Online, the relative cases of "Martha" and of "Andy" and even of "Alexis," who originally took her mother's side in the divorce, get debated with startling familiarity. "BTW, I don't blame Andy," one contributor offers. "I think he took all he could. I think it's too bad that Alexis felt she had to choose." Another contributor, another view: "I work fifty hours a week and admit sometimes I don't have time to 'be all that I can be' but when Martha started out she was doing this part-time and raising Alexis and making a home for that schmuck Andy (I bet he is sorry he ever left her)."

Although "The UNOFFICIAL Site!" is just that, unofficial, "not affiliated with Martha Stewart, her agents, Martha Stewart Living Omnimedia, LLC or any other Martha Stewart Enterprises," its fairly lighthearted approach to its subject's protean competence ("What can't Martha do? According to Martha herself, 'Hang-gliding, and I hate shopping for clothes'") should in no way be construed as disloyalty to Martha's objectives, which are, as the prospectus prepared for Martha Stewart Living Omnimedia's initial public offering last October explained, "to provide our original 'how-to' content and information to as many consumers as possible" and "to turn our consumers into 'doers' by offering them the information

and products they need for do-it-yourself ingenu-
ity 'the Martha Stewart way.'" The creators and
users of "The UNOFFICIAL Site!" clearly maintain a
special relationship with the subject at hand, as do
the creators and users of other unofficial or self-
invented sites crafted in the same spirit: "My Martha Stewart Page," say, or "Gothic Martha Stewart,"
which advises teenagers living at home on how
they can "goth up" their rooms without alarming
their parents ("First of all, don't paint everything
black") by taking their cues from Martha.

"Martha adores finding old linens and gently
worn furniture at flea markets," users of "Gothic
Martha Stewart" are reminded. "She sews a lot
of her own household dressings. She paints and
experiments with unusual painting techniques
on objects small and large. She loves flowers, live
and dried . . . and even though her surroundings
look very rich, many of her ideas are created from
rather simple and inexpensive materials, like fab-
ric scraps and secondhand dishes." For the creator
of "My Martha Stewart Page," even the "extremely
anal" quality of Martha's expressed preoccupation
with the appearance of her liquid-detergent dis-

penser can be a learning experience, a source of concern that becomes a source of illumination: "It makes me worry about her. . . . Of course it is just this strangeness that makes me love her. She helps me know I'm OK—everyone's OK. . . . She seems perfect, but she's not. She's obsessed. She's frantic. She's a control freak beyond my wildest dreams. And that shows me two things: A) no one is perfect and B) there's a price for everything."

There is an unusual bonding here, a proprietary intimacy that eludes conventional precepts of merchandising to go to the very heart of the enterprise, the brand, what Martha prefers to call the "presence": the two magazines (*Martha Stewart Living* and *Martha Stewart Weddings*) that between them reach 10 million readers, the twenty-seven books that have sold 8.5 million copies, the weekday radio show carried on 270 stations, the syndicated "AskMartha" column that appears in 233 newspapers, the televised show six days a week on CBS, the weekly slot on the CBS morning show, the cable-TV show (*From Martha's Kitchen,* the Food Network's top-rated weekly show among women aged twenty-five to fifty-four), the website (www.marthastewart.com) with more than one million registered users and 627,000 hits a month, the merchandising tie-ins with Kmart and Sears and Sherwin-Williams (Kmart alone last year sold more than a billion dollars' worth of Martha Stewart merchandise), the catalogue operation (Martha by Mail), from which some 2,800 products (Valentine Garlands, Valentine Treat Bags, Ready-to-Decorate Cookies, Sweetheart Cake Rings, Heart Dessert Scoops, Heart Rosette Sets, Heart-Shaped Pancake Molds, and Lace-Paper Valentine Kits, to name a few from the online "Valentine's Day" pages) can be ordered either from the catalogues themselves (eleven annual editions, 15 million copies) or from webpages with exceptionally inviting layouts and seductively logical links.

These products are not inexpensive. The Lace-Paper Valentine Kit contains enough card stock and paper lace to make "about forty" valentines, which could be viewed as something less than a buy at forty-two dollars plus time and labor. On the "Cakes and Cake Stands" page, the Holiday Cake-Stencil Set, which consists of eight nine-

inch plastic stencils for the decorative dusting
of cakes with confectioner's sugar or cocoa, sells
for twenty-eight dollars. On the "marthasflowers"
pages, twenty-five tea roses, which are available
for eighteen dollars a dozen at Roses Only in New
York, cost fifty-two dollars, and the larger of the
two "suggested vases" to put them in (an example
of the site's linking logic) another seventy-eight
dollars. A set of fifty Scalloped Tulle Rounds, eight-
and-three-quarter-inch circles of tulle in which to
tie up wedding favors, costs eighteen dollars, and
the seam binding used to tie them ("sold sepa-
rately," another natural link) costs, in the six-color
Seam-Binding Ribbon Collection, fifty-six dollars. Seam binding sells retail for pennies, and, at
Paron on West Fifty-seventh Street in New York,
not the least expensive source, 108-inch-wide
tulle sells for four dollars a yard. Since the amount
of 108-inch tulle required to make fifty Scalloped
Tulle Rounds would be slightly over a yard, the
online buyer can be paying only for the impri-
matur of "Martha," whose genius it was to take
the once familiar notion of doing-it-yourself to
previously uncharted territory: somewhere east

of actually doing it yourself, somewhere west of paying Robert Isabell to do it.

This is a billion-dollar company the only real product of which, in other words, is Martha Stewart herself, an unusual business condition acknowledged in the prospectus prepared for Martha Stewart Living Omnimedia's strikingly successful October IPO. "Our business would be adversely affected if: Martha Stewart's public image or reputation were to be tarnished," the "Risk Factors" section of the prospectus read in part. "Martha Stewart, as well as her name, her image, and the trademarks and other intellectual property rights relating to these, are integral to our marketing efforts and form the core of our brand name. Our continued success and the value of our brand name therefore depends, to a large degree, on the reputation of Martha Stewart."

The perils of totally identifying a brand with a single living and therefore vulnerable human being were much discussed around the time of the IPO, and the question of what would happen to Martha Stewart Living Omnimedia if Martha Stewart were to become ill or die ("the diminution or loss of the services of Martha Stewart," in the words of the prospectus) remained open. "That was always an issue for us," Don Logan, the president of Time Inc., told the *Los Angeles Times* in 1997, a few months after Stewart managed to raise enough of what she called "internally generated capital," $53.3 million, to buy herself out of Time Warner, which had been resisting expansion of a business built entirely around a single personality. "I think we are now spread very nicely over an area where our information can be trusted," Stewart herself maintained, and it did seem clear that the very expansion and repetition of the name that had made Time Warner nervous—every "Martha Stewart" item sold, every "Martha Stewart Everyday" commercial aired—was paradoxically serving to insulate the brand from the possible loss of the personality behind it.

The related question, of what would happen if "Martha Stewart's public image or reputation were to be tarnished," seemed less worrisome, since in any practical way the question of whether it was possible to tarnish Martha Stewart's public image or reputation had already been answered, with the 1997 publication and ascension to the *New York Times* best-seller list of *Just Desserts,* an unauthorized biography of Martha Stewart by Jerry Oppenheimer, whose previous books were unauthorized biographies of Rock Hudson, Barbara Walters, and Ethel Kennedy. "My investigative juices began to flow," Oppenheimer wrote in the preface to *Just Desserts.* "If her stories were true, I foresaw a book about a perfect woman who had brought perfection to the masses. If her stories were not true, I foresaw a book that would shatter myths."

Investigative juices flowing, Oppenheimer discovered that Martha was "driven." Martha, moreover, sometimes "didn't tell the whole story." Martha could be "a real screamer" when situations did not go as planned, although the case Oppenheimer makes on this point suggests, at worst, merit on both sides. Martha was said to have "started to shriek," for example, when a catering partner backed a car over the "picture-perfect" Shaker picnic basket she had just finished packing with her own blueberry pies. Similarly, Martha was said to have been "just totally freaked" when a smokehouse fire interrupted the shooting of a holiday special and she found that the hose she had personally dragged to the smokehouse ("followed by various blasé crew people, faux-concerned family members, smirking kitchen assistants, and a macho Brazilian groundskeeper") was too short to reach the flames. After running back to the house, getting an extension for the hose, and putting out the fire, Martha, many would think understandably, exchanged words with the groundskeeper, "whom she fired on the spot in front of everyone after he talked back to her."

Other divined faults include idealizing her early family life (p. 34), embellishing "everything" (p. 42), omitting a key ingredient when a rival preteen caterer asked for her chocolate-cake recipe (p. 43), telling readers of *Martha Stewart Living* that she had as a young girl "sought to discover the key to good literature" even though "a close friend" reported that she had "passionately devoured" the Nancy Drew and Cherry Ames

novels (p. 48), misspelling "villainous" in a review
of William Makepeace Thackeray's *Vanity Fair*
for the Nutley High School literary magazine
(p. 51), having to ask what Kwanza was during a
1995 appearance on *Larry King Live* (p. 71), and
not only wanting a larger engagement diamond
than the one Andy had picked out for her at Harry
Winston but obtaining it, at a better price, in the
diamond district (p. 101). "That should have set off
an alarm," a "lifelong friend" told Oppenheimer.
"How many women would do something like
that? It was a bad omen."

This lumping together of insignificant imma-
turities and economies for conversion into character flaws (a former assistant in the catering
business Martha ran in Westport during the 1970s
presents the damning charge "Nothing went to
waste. . . . Martha's philosophy was like someone at
a restaurant who had eaten half his steak and tells
the waiter 'Oh, wrap it up, and I'll take it home' ")
continues for 414 pages, at which point Oppenheimer, in full myth-shattering mode, reveals his
trump card, "an eerie corporate manifesto" that
"somehow slipped out of Martha's offices and

made its way from one Time Inc. executive's desk to another and eventually from a Xerox machine to the outside world. . . . The white paper, replete with what was described as an incomprehensible flow chart, declared, in part":

> In Martha's vision, the shared value of the MSL enterprises are highly personal—reflecting her individual goals, beliefs, values and aspirations. . . . "Martha's Way" can be obtained because she puts us in direct touch with everything we need to know, and tells/shows us exactly what we have to do. . . . MSL enterprises are founded on the proposition that Martha herself is both leader and teacher. . . . While the ranks of "teaching disciples" within MSL may grow and extend, their authority rests on their direct association with Martha; their work emanates from her approach and philosophies; and their techniques, and products and results meet her test. . . . The magazine, books, television series, and other distribution sources are only vehicles to enable personal com-

munication with Martha. . . . She is not, and
won't allow herself to be, an institutional
image and fiction like Betty Crocker. . . . She
is the creative and driving center. . . . By listening to Martha and following her lead, we
can achieve real results in our homes too—
ourselves—just like she has. . . . It is easy to
do. Martha has already "figured it out." She
will personally take us by the hand and show
us how to do it.

Oppenheimer construes this purloined memo
or mission statement as sinister, of a piece with
the Guyana Kool-Aid massacre ("From its word-
ing, some wondered whether Martha's world
was more gentrified Jonestown than happy
homemaker"), but in fact it remains an unexcep-
tionable, and quite accurate, assessment of what
makes the enterprise go. Martha Stewart Living
Omnimedia LLC connects on a level that tran-
scends the absurdly labor-intensive and in many
cases prohibitively expensive table settings and
decorating touches (the "poinsettia wreath made
entirely of ribbon" featured on one December

show would require of even a diligent maker, Martha herself allowed, "a couple of hours" and, "if you use the very best ribbon, two or three hundred dollars") over which its chairman toils six mornings a week on CBS. Nor is the connection about her recipes, which are the recipes of Sunbelt Junior League cookbooks (Grapefruit Mimosas, Apple Cheddar Turnovers, and Southwestern Style S'Mores are a few from the most recent issue of *Martha Stewart Entertaining*), reflecting American middle-class home cooking as it has existed pretty much through the postwar years. There is in a Martha Stewart recipe none of, say, Elizabeth David's transforming logic and assurance, none of Julia Child's mastery of technique.

What there is instead is "Martha," full focus, establishing "personal communication" with the viewer or reader, showing, telling, leading, teaching, "loving it" when the simplest possible shaken-in-a-jar vinaigrette emulsifies right there onscreen. She presents herself not as an authority but as the friend who has "figured it out," the enterprising if occasionally manic neighbor who will waste no opportunity to share an educational footnote. "True," or "Ceylon," cinnamon, the reader of *Martha Stewart Living* will learn, "originally came from the island now called Sri Lanka," and "by the time of the Roman Empire ... was valued at fifteen times its weight in silver." In a television segment about how to serve champagne, Martha will advise her viewers that the largest champagne bottle, the Balthazar, was named after the king of Babylon, "555 to 539 B.C." While explaining how to decorate the house for the holidays around the theme "The Twelve Days of Christmas," Martha will slip in this doubtful but nonetheless useful gloss, a way for the decorator to perceive herself as doing something more significant than painting pressed-paper eggs with two or three coats of white semigloss acrylic paint, followed by another two or three coats of yellow-tinted acrylic varnish, and finishing the result with ribbon and beads: "With the egg so clearly associated with new life, it is not surprising that the six geese a-laying represented the six days of Creation in the carol."

.   .   .

The message Martha is actually sending, the reason large numbers of American women count
watching her a comforting and obscurely inspi-
rational experience, seems not very well understood. There has been a flurry of academic work
done on the cultural meaning of her success (in
the summer of 1998, *The New York Times* reported
that "about two dozen scholars across the United
States and Canada" were producing such studies
as "A Look at Linen Closets: Liminality, Structure
and Anti-Structure in Martha Stewart Living"
and locating "the fear of transgression" in the
magazine's "recurrent images of fences, hedges
and garden walls"), but there remains, both in the
bond she makes and in the outrage she provokes,
something unaddressed, something pitched, like
a dog whistle, too high for traditional textual
analysis. The outrage, which reaches sometimes
startling levels, centers on the misconception that
she has somehow tricked her admirers into not
noticing the ambition that brought her to their
attention. To her critics, she seems to represent a
fraud to be exposed, a wrong to be righted. "She's
a shark," one declares in *Salon*. "However much

she's got, Martha wants more. And she wants it her way and in her world, not in the balls-out boys' club realms of real estate or technology, but in the delicate land of doily hearts and wedding cakes."

"I can't believe people don't see the irony in the fact that this 'ultimate homemaker' has made a multi-million dollar empire out of baking cookies and selling bed sheets," a posting reads in *Salon*'s "ongoing discussion" of Martha. "I read an interview in *Wired* where she said she gets home at 11pm most days, which means she's obviously too busy to be the perfect mom/wife/homemaker—a role which many women feel like they have to live up to because of the image MS projects." Another reader cuts to the chase: "Wasn't there some buzz a while back about Martha stealing her daughter's BF?" The answer: "I thought that was Erica Kane. You know, when she stole Kendra's BF. I think you're getting them confused. Actually, why would any man want to date MS? She is so frigid looking that my television actually gets cold when she's on." "The trouble is that Stewart is about as genuine as Hollywood," a writer in *The Scotsman* charges. "Hers may seem to be a nostalgic siren call for a return to Fifties-style homemaking with an updated elegance, but is she in fact sending out a fraudulent message—putting pressure on American women to achieve impossible perfection in yet another sphere, one in which, unlike ordinary women, Stewart herself has legions of helpers?"

This entire notion of "the perfect mom/wife/homemaker," of the "nostalgic siren call for a return to Fifties-style homemaking," is a considerable misunderstanding of what Martha Stewart actually transmits, the promise she makes her readers and viewers, which is that know-how in the house will translate to can-do outside it. What she offers, and what more strictly professional shelter and food magazines and shows do not, is the promise of transferred manna, transferred luck. She projects a level of taste that transforms the often pointlessly ornamented details of what she is actually doing. The possibility of moving out of the perfected house and into the headier ether of executive action, of doing as Martha does, is clearly presented: "Now I, as a single human being, have six personal fax numbers, fourteen personal phone numbers, seven car-phone numbers, and two cell-phone numbers," as she told readers of *Martha Stewart Living*. On October 19, the evening of her triumphant IPO, she explained, on *The Charlie Rose Show*, the genesis of the enterprise. "I was serving a desire—not only mine, but every homemaker's desire, to elevate that job of homemaker," she said. "It was floundering, I think. And we all wanted to escape it, to get out of the house, get that high-paying job and pay somebody else to do everything that we didn't think was really worthy of our attention. And all of a sudden I realized: it was terribly worthy of our attention."

Think about this. Here was a woman who had elevated "that job of homemaker" to a level where even her GMC Suburban came equipped with a Sony MZ-B3 Minidisc Recorder for dictation and a Sony ICD-50 Recorder for short messages and a Watchman FDL-PT22 TV set, plus phones, plus PowerBook. Here was a woman whose idea of how to dress for "that job of homemaker" involved

Jil Sander. "Jil's responded to the needs of people like me," she is quoted as having said on "The UNOFFICIAL Site!" "I'm busy; I travel a lot; I want to look great in a picture." Here was a woman who had that very October morning been driven down to the big board to dispense brioches and fresh-squeezed orange juice from a striped tent while Morgan Stanley Dean Witter and Merrill Lynch and Bear Stearns and Donaldson, Lufkin & Jenrette and Banc of America Securities increased the value of her personal stock in the company she personally invented to $614 million. This does not play into any "nostalgic siren call" for a return to the kind of "homemaking" that seized America during those postwar years when the conversion of industry to peacetime production mandated the creation of a market for Kelvinators, yet Martha was the first to share the moment with her readers.

"The mood was festive, the business community receptive, and the stock began trading with the new symbol MSO," she confided in her "Letter from Martha" in the December *Martha Stewart Living,* and there between the lines was the promise from the mission statement: *It is easy to do. Martha has already "figured it out." She will personally take us by the hand and show us how to do it.* What she will show us how to do, it turns out, is a little more invigorating than your average poinsettia-wreath project: "The process was extremely interesting, from deciding exactly what the company was (an 'integrated multimedia company' with promising internet capabilities) to creating a complicated and lengthy prospectus that was vetted and revetted (only to be vetted again by the Securities and Exchange Commission) to selling the company with a road show that took us to more than twenty cities in fourteen days (as far off as Europe)." This is getting out of the house with a vengeance, and on your own terms, the secret dream of any woman who has ever made a success of a PTA cake sale. "You could bottle that chili sauce," neighbors say to home cooks all over America. "You could make a fortune on those date bars." You could bottle it, you could sell it, you can survive when all else fails: I myself believed for most of my adult life that I could support myself and my family, in the catastrophic absence of all other income sources, by catering.

The "cultural meaning" of Martha Stewart's success, in other words, lies deep in the success itself, which is why even her troubles and strivings are part of the message, not detrimental but integral to the brand. She has branded herself not as Superwoman but as Everywoman, a distinction that seems to remain unclear to her critics. Martha herself gets it, and talks about herself in print as if catching up her oldest friend. "I sacrificed family, husband," she said in a 1996 *Fortune* conversation with Charlotte Beers, the former CEO of Ogilvy & Mather and a member of Martha Stewart Living Omnimedia's board of directors, and Darla Moore, the president of Richard Rainwater's investment firm and the inventor of "debtor in possession" financing for companies in bankruptcy. The tone of this conversation was odd, considerably more confessional than the average dialogue among senior executives who know they are being taped by *Fortune.* "Not my choice," Martha confided about her divorce. "His choice. Now, I'm so happy that it happened. It took a long time for me to realize that it freed me to do more things. I don't think I would have accomplished what I have if I had stayed married.

No way. And it allowed me to make friends that I
know I never would have had."

Martha's readers understand her divorce, both its
pain and its upside. They saw her through it, just as
they saw her through her dealings with the SEC,
her twenty-city road show, her triumph on Wall
Street. This relationship between Martha and her
readers is a good deal more complicated than the
many parodies of and jokes about it would allow.
"While fans don't grow on fruit trees (well, some
do), they can be found all over America: in malls,
and Kmarts, in tract houses and trailer parks, in
raised ranches, Tudor condos and Winnebagos,"
the parody Martha is made to say in HarperCollins's *Martha Stuart's Better Than You at Entertaining.* "Wherever there are women dissatisfied
with how they live, with who they are and who
they are not, that is where you'll find potential fans
of mine." These parodies are themselves interesting: too broad, misogynistic in a cartoon way
(stripping Martha to her underwear has been a
reliable motif of countless online parodies), curi-

ously nervous ("Keeping Razors Circumcision-Sharp" is one feature in *Martha Stuart's Better Than You at Entertaining*), oddly uncomfortable, a little too intent on marginalizing a rather considerable number of women by making light of their situations and their aspirations.

Something here is perceived as threatening, and a glance at "The UNOFFICIAL Site!," the subliminal focus of which is somewhere other than on homemaking skills, suggests what it is. What makes Martha "a good role model in many ways," one contributor writes, is that "she's a strong woman who's in charge, and she has indeed changed the way our country, if not the world, views what used to be called 'women's work.'" From an eleven-year-old: "Being successful is important in life.... It is fun to say 'When I become Martha Stewart I'm going to have all the things Martha has.'" Even a contributor who admits to an "essentially anti-Martha persona" admires her "intelligence" and "drive," the way in which this "supreme chef, baker, gardener, decorator, artist, and entrepreneur" showed what it took "to get where she is, where most men aren't and can't.... She owns her own corporation in her own name, her own magazine, her own show."

A keen interest in and admiration for business acumen pervades the site. "I know people are threatened by Martha and Time Warner Inc. is going to blow a very 'good thing' if they let Martha and her empire walk in the near future," a contributor to "The UNOFFICIAL Site!" wrote at the time Stewart was trying to buy herself out of Time Warner. "I support Martha in everything she does and I would bet if a man wanted to attach his name to all he did . . . this wouldn't be a question." Their own words tell the story these readers and viewers take from Martha: Martha is *in charge,* Martha is *where most men aren't and can't,* Martha has *her own magazine,* Martha has *her own show,* Martha not only has *her own corporation* but has it *in her own name.*

This is not a story about a woman who made the best of traditional skills. This is a story about a woman who did her own IPO. This is the "woman's pluck" story, the dust-bowl story, the burying-your-child-on-the-trail story, the I-will-never-go-hungry-again story, the Mildred Pierce story, the story about how the sheer nerve of even professionally unskilled women can prevail, show the men; the story that has historically encouraged women in this country, even as it has threatened men. The dreams and the fears into which Martha Stewart taps are not of "feminine" domesticity but of female power, of the woman who sits down at the table with the men and, still in her apron, walks away with the chips.

2000

A NOTE ABOUT THE AUTHOR

Joan Didion is the author of five novels, ten books of nonfiction, and a play. She lives in New York.

A NOTE ON THE TYPE

The text of this book was set in Didot, a revival of the typefaces of the Parisian typefounder Firmin Didot (1764–1836).

Composed by North Market Street Graphics
Lancaster, Pennsylvania

Printed and bound by LSC Communications
Crawfordsville, Indiana

Designed by Maggie Hinders